# BUSINESS ADMINISTRATION
Theory and Practice

Alberto Silva

Copyright © 2022 Alberto Silva Aristeguieta

All rights reserved.

ISBN-13: 979-8-35-328441-3

# PREFACE

This book, aimed at business administration students at any level (bachelor's, master's, or doctorate), and practicing managers, is the product of a comprehensive review of the best academic literature on this field of study, supported by my managerial experience and my teaching activity for many years.

The book's chapters correspond, in general, to the courses taught in the study programs of Business Administration, for example, organizational change, organizational behavior, strategy, human resources. The subjects are in alphabetical order.

This book does not have the depth of a textbook. It is a guide or handbook to provide the student, in a few pages, with a general orientation that will facilitate the most complete study of the subject using textbooks and other support materials.

The content takes advantage of information from many sources, ignoring the academic citation rigor to facilitate reading. At the end of each chapter there is a brief list of recommended references, which allow the students to expand their knowledge on the topics covered.

THE AUTHOR

# CONTENTS

PREFACE ........................................................................ 1

CONTENTS ..................................................................... 3

1 ADMINISTRATION THEORY ................................... 5

2 BUSINESS PLAN ...................................................... 21

3 COMPANIES AND ENTREPRENEURS ..................... 29

4 DECISIONS .............................................................. 39

5 ECONOMICS ........................................................... 51

6 ETHICS AND CORPORATE SOCIAL RESPONSIBILITY 65

7 FINANCE .................................................................. 73

8 HUMAN RESOURCES .............................................. 83

9 INTERNATIONAL BUSINESS .................................... 95

10 LEADERSHIP ........................................................ 109

11 MANAGERIAL COMMUNICATION ....................... 119

| 12 | MANAGERS | 129 |
| 13 | MARKETING | 141 |
| 14 | OPERATIONS | 153 |
| 15 | ORGANIZATIONAL BEHAVIOR | 169 |
| 16 | ORGANIZATIONAL CHANGE | 185 |
| 17 | ORGANIZATIONAL DESIGN | 201 |
| 18 | PROJECT MANAGEMENT | 211 |
| 19 | STRATEGY | 221 |
| 20 | TECHNOLOGY | 235 |

# 1 ADMINISTRATION THEORY

## 1.1 THEORIES OF ADMINISTRATION

Administration or management theories, also called organization theory, refer to a set of approaches that try to explain and predict how organizations or companies can obtain better results.

There is no single enumeration of the various theories of management or administration or a universally accepted classification of them; however, the following theories are frequently mentioned:

- Classical theories of management.
- Human relations theory.
- Systems approach.
- Contingency theory.
- Economic theories of the company.
- Organizational design theory.
- Strategic theory of the company.

Information on organizational design theory and strategic enterprise theory are in chapters 17 (Organizational Design) and 19 (Strategy) of this book. Below there are comments on the other theories mentioned.

## 1.2 THE CLASSICAL THEORIES OF MANAGEMENT

The theories proposed in the first decades of the twentieth century by Frederick Taylor in the United States (scientific direction of work), Henri Fayol in France (school of the administrative process), and Max Weber in Germany (bureaucratic school), were the first modern attempts to establish some principles that would help managers to understand how companies operate and apply that knowledge to improve their performance.

### 1.2.1 The similarities and differences among the early theorists of management

Taylor, Fayol, and Weber agreed on the method used: observe what was happening in companies, describe it, analyze it, and propose recommendations for improvement. However, they differed in the scope and purpose of their investigations:

Taylor focused on work processes, with the purpose of improving the productivity and efficiency of those processes.

Fayol focused on the functions of managers, with the purpose of helping them better understand their functions and apply principles that would allow them to achieve a better performance of the organization

Weber analyzed the structure and rules that characterize the proper functioning of organizations.

Both Fayol and Weber based their theories on the observation of bureaucratic organizations, which were the prevailing organizations in their time.

### 1.2.2  The legacy of the first authors

The three mentioned authors laid the foundations for the future development of management studies, each from their own perspective:

Taylor was the forerunner of industrial engineering and operations research (management science), as well as all actions aimed at improving work processes, such as total quality and reengineering.

Fayol was the first to establish the functions of managers and to analyze how their relationships with employees should be for the best functioning of the company, an effort continued by scholars of management in general and organizational behavior in particular.

Weber, on the other hand, was the initiator of the studies of the sociology of organizations, oriented to analyze how the members of an organization build and coordinate organized collective activities.

Each of the currents initiated by these authors has had an independent development, although there are efforts to integrate these actions.

## 1.3  THE THEORY OF HUMAN RELATIONS

The theory of human relations is the set of efforts made in the first decades of the twentieth century to analyze and highlight the importance of human aspects in the operation of companies.

### 1.3.1  The origin of the theory of human relations

The main contribution of the school or theory of human relations, initiated in 1933 by Elton Mayo, was to raise awareness about the importance of human aspects in the management of companies. Although some authors, such as Henri Fayol and Mary Parker Follett, had previously stressed the importance of good human relations for the running of a company, the experiments conducted by Mayo and its subsequent theoretical conception demonstrated unequivocally that people are not machines or simple resources of production, but if treated as human beings they could work more at ease and perform better. Fayol was French and his work was not known or valued in the United States until long after published in France and Follett, although American, was a social worker, and she could not access to Harvard because was a woman. Mayo, on the other hand, was a Harvard professor and in conducting Hawthorne's studies his findings quickly gained fame. From the theory of human relations, companies understood that they depended on human talent and the working conditions of employees improved a lot in the second half of the last century.

### 1.3.2 The importance of informal relations between workers

Apart from highlighting the importance of people in the productivity of enterprises, human relations theory also underlined the importance of informal relationships. Until that time, there was the idea that only vertical formal relationships, that is, orders issued by superiors to subordinates, were of importance in the productive process. Hawthorne's experiments made it possible to recognize that informal relationships between employees, apart from hierarchical relationships between bosses and employees, could exert a lot of influence on the behavior and performance of workers.

### 1.3.3 The study of organizational behavior

The concern for the human aspects of work in companies gave rise to a current of study that continues to this day as organizational behavior, covering topics such as motivation, commitment, teamwork, conflict management, human resources management, power and politics in organizations, and leadership. Topics of organizational behavior are in this book in chapters 8 (Human Resources), 10 (Leadership), and 15 (Organizational Behavior).

### 1.3.4 The problems of people in companies

Unfortunately, in this century (despite the business discourse on the importance of people) people live under excessive pressure to achieve more results, work long hours, and companies fire or threaten them with dismissal if things do not go well in the opinion of managers (even if it is because of themselves). Studies conducted in different countries on job satisfaction show that most employees are not happy in the organization in which they work and if they had the opportunity they would go to another organization.

## 1.4 THE SYSTEMS APPROACH

### 1.4.1 The organization as a system

The visualization of organization as a system emerged at the beginning of the second half of the twentieth century, when many fields of human activity received the influence of systems theory. There is no doubt that the systems approach was a breakthrough for the understanding of many natural and social phenomena. It is an example of how a simple idea can have a major impact on science and how it can be useful to transfer knowledge from one science to another, in this case from biology to other sciences.

Seeing the company as a system, instead of considering it composed of isolated parts, and particularly as an open system, that is, in interaction with the environment and not closed to it, has helped a lot to understand it better. More recently, visualizing global companies as complex systems, that is, composed of many parts, has also allowed them to apply the knowledge acquired in other areas on the management of complexity.

### 1.4.2 The components of the company's system

The parts of the business organization are employees, managers, equipment, machines, systems, and rules and procedures, but also intangible ones, such as culture and essential competencies (what people and the organization know how to do well). All those parts interact with each other and with the environment to achieve the organization's goals.

In addition to this definition of the components of

the organization, known as the 7S or McKinsey model, there are several analogies to understand the functioning of the organization as a system, comparing it with a machine, a brain, an entity of flow and transformation, a culture, a political system, or an organism.

### 1.4.3 Strategy is the fundamental element of the system

For the company's system to work well, there must be harmony between all its components. In general, strategy is the starting point, since it defines what objectives you want to achieve and what type of company you must have to achieve those objectives. The other components must harmonize with strategy.

## 1.5 THE CONTINGENCY THEORY

Contingency theory, developed in the 1960s, proposed that there is nothing absolute or permanent in the functioning of organizations but that it depends on the contingencies or circumstances of the environment. Contingency theory makes use of the notion of organization as a system, particularly as an open system, analyzing the relationship of the organization with its environment. According to this theory, the best way to organize depends on the nature of the environment with which an organization interacts.

At the beginning of contingency theory, biological similes still prevailed to analyze systems. In living beings, their structure is closely related to the environment. The evolution of humans, affected by changes or contingencies in the environment in which they lived, led early contingency theorists to analyze the relationship between the structure of organizations and their environment; however, very soon they realized, from the contributions of Alfred Chandler, that the structure was really a consequence of the strategy and that it was this that depended on the environment.

## 1.6 THE ECONOMIC THEORIES OF THE COMPANY

### 1.6.1 The neoclassical theory of the enterprise

The so-called neoclassical theory of the enterprise, proposed after the Second World War and promoted by authors such as Peter Drucker, famous economist, consultant, and author of management books during the second half of the twentieth century, considers this as the unit of elementary production, maximizing profit, which acts as a demander of productive factors and, in turn, offeror of goods and services.

This school of thought has focused on the study of the functioning of markets and the formation of prices. Neoclassical assumptions about the company, including the assumption of perfect competition, have made this model the subject of much criticism and today has only historical value.

### 1.6.2 The industrial economy

The industrial economy approach abandoned the hypothesis of perfect competition of the neoclassical model, seeking to discern the behavior of firms by analyzing the type of decisions made by firms in contexts of imperfect competition and determining when this harm efficiency. Industrial economics analyzes the interdependencies of firms within markets and studies market conditions, firm behavior, and economic outcomes.

### 1.6.3 The new institutional economy

The new institutional economy, developed from the decade of the nineties of the last century, studied the historical conditions in which institutions arise and the analysis of their mechanisms of organization or government. Within the framework of the new institutional economy, three approaches or perspectives of the economic analysis of organizations emerged:

- **The economics of transaction costs**, defined as those incurred for conducting the exchange of a good or service and for monitoring compliance with the agreement. A typical example is the cost of lawyers involved in an agreement between two companies.
- **The economics of property rights**. According to this approach, people's rights over resources take on their own entity as a basic prerequisite of all economic activity.
- **The theory of agency**. It is based on the agency relationship, defined as an explicit or implicit contract, between two parties, by which one of them, called an agent, undertakes to perform a certain activity, or provide a service on behalf of the other, called the principal. In any agency relationship there is a risk of deviation from the agent's conduct from the interests of the principal and, therefore, every time the principal delegates authority to the agent and the problem arises of how to efficiently monitor is or her conduct.

### 1.6.4 Evolutionary economic theory

Evolutionary economic theory, developed by Richard Nelson and Sidney Winter from 1982, unlike the previous economic theories of the company, incorporated the dynamic element into the economic analysis of organizations. This approach gave rise to the concept of the dynamic capacities of the organization and the theory of resources and capacities, analyzed in chapter 19 of this book (Strategy).

## 1.7 MANAGEMENT THEORY AND PRACTICE

Management theory and practice do not always go hand in hand. Some authors think this is due to the difficulty of testing managerial theories before putting them into practice. However, most managers are not concerned with the empirical proof of theories and therefore that is not usually the reason for the gap between management theory and practice.

As far as the application of theories in the practice of management is concerned, it is necessary to distinguish between theories related to human behavior and theories related to the optimization of the use of resources.

### 1.7.1 Organizational behavior theories and management practice

Theories related to human behavior, corresponding in general to the field of organizational behavior, insist that people feel more satisfied with their work and are more productive if managers trust them and give polite treatment to them, let them participate in crucial decisions, recognize their work, and allow them a good degree of autonomy and initiative to perform it. However, in practice most managers distrust and treat their subordinates badly, do not take them into account for decisions, do not recognize their work, and allow them little or no initiative to do. It is difficult to determine the causes of this misconduct in many managers, but it is due to ignorance and inherited prejudices about what the relationships between managers and subordinates should be.

### 1.7.2 Quantitative theories and management practice

As for the theories related to the optimization of resources, corresponding in general to operations research, the lack of application of these may be due to the ignorance of many managers and their lack of sufficient mathematical and statistical knowledge to allow them to understand and apply these theories.

### 1.7.3 The need to understand and apply management theories

Managers must develop the ability to understand and apply management theories in their work, as this can make things much easier for them and avoid making costly mistakes. They should not only focus on learning how companies succeed but also learning from failures. Managers, when facing a problem, must know how to identify which theory can help them and how to distinguish a good theory from a bad one.

### 1.7.4 Management journals and books

The Harvard Business Review is a good guide to identifying and applying theoretical knowledge. There are other peer-reviewed journals (for example, Academy of Management, Sloan Management Review, Organizational Science, Strategic Management Journal, Journal of Management, Journal of International Business Studies, and Journal of Marketing), but unfortunately most managers find the papers published in those journals very abstract, and difficult to turn into practical actions. In any case, students or managers should not use "best-sellers" of very dubious scientific quality.

## 1.8 RECOMMENDED READING

- Daft, R.L. (2020). Organization theory and design. Cengage Learning, 13th Edition.
- Hendry, J. (2013). Management: A very short introduction. Oxford University Press.
- Rodriguez, C. A. (2001). Fayol's 14 principles of management then and now: a framework for managing today's organizations effectively. Management Decision, 2001; 39, 10, pp. 880-889.
- Wigzell, M. (2016). A history of management thought. Routledge, 2nd Edition.

# 2 BUSINESS PLAN

## 2.1 THE BUSINESS PLAN

A business plan is an analysis document for making decisions on how to implement an idea, initiative, or business project. This document should present in detail the development and monitoring of a business opportunity to financial institutions, banks, or partners.

## 2.2 THE PURPOSE OF THE BUSINESS PLAN

A business plan is essential to support a loan application that allows you to start a business, but it is much more than that: it is a guide to help the entrepreneurs define and achieve their goals. The business plan shows where a company will go, how it will get there, and what it will be like when it arrives.

A business plan should serve, at least, to:

- Set goals and objectives.
- Provide a foundation for monitoring company performance.
- Communicate the company's message to its stakeholders.

A business plan will not automatically make any

entrepreneurial initiative a success, but it will help you avoid some common causes of failure, such as decapitalization or lack of a suitable market.

## 2.3   THE STRUCTURE OF A BUSINESS PLAN

Although there are many guides or models for structuring a business plan, there is freedom to structure it in the most convenient way.

A model for structuring the business plan of a company are the recommendations of the U.S. Small Business Administration (SBA), transcribed verbatim as follows:

- **Executive summary.** Simply put, tell your reader what your company is and why it will succeed. State the objectives, your product or service and basic information about the management team, employees, and location of the company. Also include financial information and high-level growth plans if you plan to apply for financing.
- **Description of the company.** Provide detailed information about your company. Go into detail about the problems it solves. Be specific and mention which consumers, organizations, or companies you would serve. Explain the competitive advantages that will make your business a

success. Are there experts on your team? Did you find the ideal location for your store? This section is the place to show off your strengths.
- **Market analysis.** You will need a good understanding of the landscape of your sector and the target market. Competitive research will reveal to you what other companies do and their strengths. In your market research look for trends and topics. What do successful competitors do? Why does it work for them? Could you do better?
- **Organization and management.** Explain the structure of your company and who will run it. Describe the legal structure of your company. Indicate whether you have or intend to integrate it as a C or S corporation, form a general or limited partnership, or if you are a sole proprietorship or limited liability company. Submit an organizational chart with the names of those in charge; indicate how the experience of each will contribute to the success of your project. Consider including resumes and CVs from key team members.
- **Lines of services or products.** Describe what you sell or the service you offer. Explain how it benefits your customers and what the product

lifecycle is like. Share your plans regarding intellectual property, such as copyright or patent registrations. If you do research and development of your service or product, explain it in detail.
- **Advertising and sales.** You should describe the procedure for attracting and retaining customers, and for producing a sale. Because you will consult this section when making financial projections, try to describe in detail your complete advertising and sales strategies.
- **Request for funding.** If you are looking for financing, here you should outline your needs. Your goal is to clearly explain how much you will need in the next five years and the use you will give it. Specify whether you prefer debt or equity, the terms you want to apply for, and the period your request will cover. Provide a detailed description of how you will use your funds. Specify whether you need funds to purchase equipment or materials, pay salaries, or cover specific bills until earnings increase. Always include a description of your future strategic financial plans, such as paying off debt or selling your business.
- **Financial projections.** Supplement your request for funds with financial projections. Your goal is

to convince the reader that your company is stable and will be a financial success. If your company already exists, include income statements, balance sheets, and cash flows for the past three to five years. If you have another collateral with which to back up a loan, it is time to mention it. Give a financial prospection for the next five years. Include income statements, balance sheets, cash flows, and capital expenditure budgets. For the first year, be even more specific and use quarterly or even monthly projections. Clearly explain your projections and relate them to your funding requests. It is a suitable place to include charts and diagrams of your company's financial history.

- **Appendix.** Use your appendix to provide supporting documents or other materials requested. Include Items such as credit history, CVs, product images, reference letters, licenses, permits or patents, legal documents, and other contracts.

## 2.4  RISKS IN THE PREPARATION OF BUSINESS PLANS

Unfortunately, many business plans are not well

crafted and therefore do not fulfill their mission of facilitating the success of a business initiative. Most of these plans present too many numbers that are not relevant to smart decision-making and, in addition, are too optimistic. On the other hand, a business plan cannot be a carefully crafted prediction of the future but a description of the events that may occur and a map for the adjustments that may be necessary if things do not go as planned.

Among the main recommendations for developing a business plan, entrepreneurs should:

- Identify the necessary people. Having the right people is more important than a right business idea, because almost any business idea can fail. Without the right people, you simply cannot create a great company.
- Set short-term goals instead of long-term (more than a year) and modify the plan as your business progresses. Often long-term planning becomes insignificant due to the reality of the business, which may be different from your initial concept.
- Avoid over-optimism. To do this, you must be extremely conservative in predicting capital requirements, deadlines, sales, and profits. Few business plans correctly anticipate how much money and time the company will require

- Grow slowly. Slow growth helps to develop good management.
- Determine what the responses will be in case of commercial adversities.
- Use simple language when explaining problems. Develop the plan so that it is easy to read and understand.
- Do not depend entirely on the exclusivity of your business or a patented invention.

## 2.5 RECOMMENDED READING

- Harvard Business Review (2014). Creating business plans. Harvard Business Review Press, 20-minute manager series.
- Sahlman, W. (1997). How to write a great business plan. Harvard Business Review, July- August 1997, pp. 98-108.
- SBA (2020). Small business guide. U.S. Small Business Administration.

# 3 COMPANIES AND ENTREPRENEURS

## 3.1 COMPANIES

A company is an organization, composed of human, material, and technical elements, which aims to obtain profits through its participation in the market for goods and services.

There are so many types of companies and so much diversity in their characteristics that it is difficult for us to imagine what they can have in common. Companies range from a small shop in a secluded village to a large corporation engaged in oil production, car manufacturing or the sale of goods around the world.

Companies varies according to different criteria:
- The legal form.
- The type of activity.
- The economic sector in which they conduct their activity.
- The size.
- The nature of the property.
- The scope of its activities.
- Membership or not in a group of companies.

## 3.1.1 Classification of companies according to legal form

According to their legal form, most of the major companies are corporations, in which the capital guarantees the obligations of the company, and the partners are bound only by the amount of their shares. However, there are other legal forms, which differ in terms of the responsibilities of their owners or partners. These different legal forms vary from country to country. In the United States, for example, apart from C corporations, or simply corporations, there are:

- Sole proprietor.
- Partnerships.
- Limited liability partnerships.
- Limited partnerships.
- Corporations S.
- Limited liability companies.
- Professional limited liability companies.
- Professional corporations.
- Non-profit partnerships.

## 3.1.2 Classification of companies according to the type of activity

Depending on the type of activity they conduct,

there are industrial, commercial, and service companies:

- Industrial companies transform raw materials into finished products for individual or industrial consumption.
- Commercial companies dedicate themselves to the purchase and sale of products.
- Service companies do not produce or market goods but offer their services to other companies or to the public.

However, there are companies that only own or hold shares of other companies, without conducting any specific activity.

### 3.1.3 Classification of companies according to the economic sector in which they conduct their activity

According to the economic sector in which they conduct their activity, we have agricultural, mining, construction, manufacturing, transport, communications, energy, services, and technology companies, among others.

### 3.1.4 Classification of companies by size

Another classification criterion of companies is size. The size of the company depends on the number of employees, the volume of sales or the combination of both factors. So, we have micro, small, medium, and large enterprises, although there are no universal criteria to differentiate one from the other. In many countries, microenterprises are understood to be those with fewer than 10 workers, small those with between 11 and 49, medium those with between 50 and 250, and large those with more than 250; but in the United States there is not the same distinction, and it differs only between small and large companies, being the official limit of workers of a small company generally 500, although it varies between 10 and 1500 depending on the type of industry to which the company belongs. The largest companies, with hundreds of thousands of workers, have so far been car manufacturing companies, oil companies, large industrial groups or conglomerates, and companies engaged in the sale of goods around the world.

### 3.1.5 Classification of companies according to the nature of ownership

We can also distinguish companies according to the nature of their ownership. According to this criterion, we must distinguish between privately owned enterprises, State enterprises, and joint ventures (owned by both the State and private individuals or enterprises). Additionally, private and joint ventures could be closed capital companies (subscribed only by the partners) or open capital companies (with shares offered on the stock markets). Open capital companies are public in the United States, but in other countries public companies are State-owned enterprises.

The problem with public or open capital companies is that managers run them with short-term criteria, to preserve or increase the value of the shares and prevent shareholders from withdrawing and selling their shares. Some authors think that managers of public companies should run them with long-term interests, such as a scheme of shares owned by employees or one or more pension funds.

### 3.1.6 Classification of companies according to the scope of their activities

According to the scope of their activities, companies could be local, national, international, multinational, or global:

- Local businesses are those that operate only in one city or area of a country.

- National companies operate throughout the territory of a country.
- International companies operate in more than one country but export their products or services from a single country.
- Multinational companies conduct production, distribution, and marketing activities in several countries.
- Global companies operate worldwide or at least in major global markets (United States, Europe, and China).

### 3.1.7 Classification of companies according to whether they belong to a group

Finally, you can distinguish between independent companies and groups of companies or corporations. Within the latter, and in accordance with its position within the group, we have the parent company and the affiliated companies or subsidiaries.

## 3.2 ENTREPRENEURS

Companies are born by the will of entrepreneurs. Sometimes the entrepreneur is a professional; for example, a lawyer who practices his profession through his own company, in this case a law firm.

However, in most cases it is simply a person or a group of people who want to start a business, having or not previous experience or training in the activity they plan to develop.

### 3.2.1 The difference between entrepreneurs and other people

Many people can generate business ideas. What sets entrepreneurs apart from anyone else is their ability to transform those ideas into reality. Entrepreneurs must be able to transform a business idea into a business plan or concept clear and specific to the product or service to offer. Once entrepreneurs define the business plan, they must have access to experience and the necessary sources of financing (partners, banks) to transform that concept into reality.

### 3.2.2 Successful entrepreneurs

Successful entrepreneurs:
- Can recognize the challenges they face.
- Believe in what they are doing.
- Find their own way of doing things.
- Develop an appropriate vision of their business.
- Show great determination and perseverance in achieving their goals.

- Have little fear of failure.
- Are comfortable with ambiguity and uncertainty.
- Know how to act at the right time. For example, some entrepreneurs take too long to start selling their product, thereby losing the opportunity to receive valuable feedback from consumers in the product design phase.

### 3.2.3 Entrepreneurs and managers

It is one thing to be an entrepreneur and another to be a manager, although in many companies these roles are confused. An entrepreneur concentrates on initiating changes and uses the factors of production to create new businesses. A manager is an administrator and concentrates on running a business to get the desired results from it. It is possible that in small businesses, the entrepreneur or owner who has created a business can also take care of its operation, but there is more awareness that management is a profession. Many companies fail because of the inability of their owners to recognize that they must entrust management to truly trained people.

## 3.3 RECOMMENDED READING

- Handy, C. (2002). What is business for? Harvard Business Review, December 2002, pp. 49-56.
- Harvard Business Review (2018). Entrepreneur's handbook: Everything you need to launch and grow your new business. Harvard Business Review Press.
- Martin, R. L. (2021). It's time to replace the public corporation. Harvard Business Review, January-February 2021, pp. 34- 42.
- Westhead, P. & Wright, M. (2014). Entrepreneurship: A very short introduction. Oxford University Press.

# 4 DECISIONS

## 4.1 THE DECISIONS

Decisions are choices between two or more alternatives to achieve something or solve a problem.

## 4.2 MANAGEMENT DECISIONS

Managers must make many decisions:

- Defining objectives, goals, and strategies.
- Initiating and directing new projects to improve the performance of the organization.
- Managing crisis and emergency situations.
- Hiring, promoting, compensating, and firing people.
- Allocating human, material, and economic resources to different activities.
- Negotiating with clients and other units of the company.

Manager's decisions could make possible to achieve the objectives of the companies and induce positive behavior of the employees but could also fail to get that. If people do not have confidence in the ability of managers to make decisions and if they do not participate in the decision-making process, it will affect the organizational climate.

Leaders who build large companies rarely suffer from indecision. The ability to decide; that is, deciding even in the absence of perfect information (which is always the case), is an essential attribute for the proper functioning of a company.

## 4.2.1  Types of decisions

There are different criteria to classify decisions. One of these criteria divides them into:

- **Programmed decisions**: repetitive and routine decisions, for which there is a defined procedure to resolve or address them.
- **Unprogrammed decisions**: novel decisions, for which there is no defined procedure to resolve or address them.

Naturally, the toughest decisions are unprogrammed, such as those related to many crises and emergency situations and those that have to do with unforeseen ethical dilemmas. But some programmed or routine decisions can also be difficult and critical, such as selecting an employee from a list of eligible candidates or promoting someone to a key position among several candidates.

According to another criterion, business decisions

could be decisions under certainty, decisions under uncertainty, or decisions at risk:

- **Decisions under certainty**, exceedingly rare, are those in which there is complete information about all the alternatives and the results are known for sure
- **Decisions under uncertainty** are those in which the results depend on conditions beyond the control of the decision maker and the probabilities of occurrence of those conditions are unknown
- **Decisions at risk** are those in which conditions beyond the control of the decision maker affect the outcomes, but the probabilities of occurrence of those conditions could be known or estimated

### 4.2.2 Methods of analysis for decision-making

In decisions under certainty, to make the best decision you simply choose the decision criterion (for example, the net profit) and choose the alternative that best meets that criterion.

For the analysis of decisions under uncertainty or minimal risk, there are qualitative and quantitative methods or techniques.

Qualitative techniques include:

- Analysis of qualitative scenarios.
- Analysis of similar cases.
- Methods of consulting individuals (surveys, Delphi technique).

Quantitative techniques include:
- Quantitative analysis of multiple scenarios (using Monte Carlo methods, decision analysis techniques, analysis of real options).
- Utility theory.
- Decision trees.
- Theory of preference.
- Game theory.

### 4.2.3 Biases in decision-making

There is the possibility of biases in a decision, due to the use of incorrect information or misinterpretation of problems. These biases are more likely to occur when conditions of elevated risk and uncertainty prevail.

Biases in decision-making can be due to:
- Thinking that the problem that occurs is like a previous one.
- Discarding information that may be useful to better understand the problem.

- Assuming that a few known cases may be representative of a larger population.
- Rushing to make the decision without thoroughly analyzing all the factors involved.
- Being risk averse.
- Being overconfident.
- Possessing prejudice against changes in the status quo.

The main defense against biases in decision-making is to be honest with yourself and think about the possibility that biases are affecting decision analysis. It also helps to know our prejudices, learn from mistakes, and seek the opinion of others, preferably those who are not directly involved in the problem.

### 4.2.4 Intuition

Many executives rely on their instinct or intuition to decide, especially when confronting the most critical decisions. Although this way of proceeding can be risky, it is also true that some people manage to develop good intuition skills, particularly those managers with a more varied and diverse experience.

The best decision makers usually combine analytical techniques with intuition. In general, analytical techniques are better in decisions under certainty or minimal risk and intuition is better in decisions under uncertainty and significant risk. Intuition has little value if decision makers could implement effective analytical techniques, but it can be extremely useful in many business decisions under uncertainty, such as those concerning strategy, investments, or people-related issues.

## 4.3 EFFECTIVE DECISIONS

### 4.3.1 Errors in decision-making

Manager's job is to make decisions. However, it is not easy to make good decisions. Many people make wrong fundamental decisions for their lives; in the same way, many managers make bad decisions in the exercise of their activities, usually with adverse consequences for other people and for the company in which they work.

Making decisions is a manager's most important job, but it is also easy to get it wrong. That is why effective managers:

- Do not make many decisions.
- Concentrate on what is important.
- Know when a decision is to be based on principles and when to be pragmatic depending on the circumstances of each case.

- Know that decision-making has its own systematic process and its own clearly defined elements.

In general, effective managers do not see decisions as a competition in which they must emerge victorious but as a collaborative process of problem solving. Nor do they think that their decisions will always be correct; in the business world the important thing is to know how to learn from mistakes.

### 4.3.2 Risks in decision-making

Managers need to make risky decisions to create value for those interested in the company; however, managers in many large corporations routinely dismiss risky ideas in favor of marginal improvements, cost reductions, or "safe" investments. This risk aversion leads to the loss of many opportunities, so managers should evaluate projects or investment options together, considering both their expected value and their risk profile and adopting a portfolio of projects with lower risk than that associated with individual projects. Middle managers should clearly expose risks to senior management, separating people from risks.

### 4.3.3 Group decisions

In general, groups make better decisions than

individuals. An advantage of group decision-making is that it can facilitate both the identification of risks and the generation of creative and innovative solutions, as well as the implementation of decisions, since the people who participated in the process will be more willing to collaborate in its execution. However, group decisions require more time, and the search for consensus or the influence of a participant can affect the decision or result in no one being responsible for a decision.

### 4.3.4   Good decision-making practices

Although there is no method that ensures you always make correct decisions, it may be best not to rush into making a major decision, consult the people you believe can help you make a good decision, and think carefully about the consequences of each option or alternative that is under consideration. Managers with good judgment tend to be good listeners and readers, able to hear what other people really think, and therefore able to see what others do not see.

It is difficult to assess a manager's judgment and only considering results could lead to wrong evaluations. It is better to consider the components that lead to good judgment:

- Learning.

- Confidence.
- Experience.
- Impartiality.
- Search for options.
- Execution.

Companies can help their managers make better decisions:

- Identifying and prioritizing the needed decisions.
- Examining the factors involved in each decision.
- Designing roles, processes, systems, and behaviors to improve decisions.
- Institutionalizing the decision process through training, refined data analysis, and evaluation of results.

### 4.3.5 Improving decision-making to drive innovation

Many companies that want to be innovative have a tough time moving fast to implement innovative ideas, due to their outdated and inefficient approaches to decision-making. Companies need to strengthen and accelerate their creative decision-making processes by including diverse perspectives, defining better processes, adjusting the pace of decisions to the pace of learning, and developing better service practices for end users.

## 4.4 RECOMMENDED READING

- Davenport, T.H. (2009). Make better decisions. Harvard Business Review, November 2009, pp. 117-123.
- Drucker, P. F. (1967). The effective decision. Harvard Business Review, January- February 1967, pp. 92-98.
- Fischhoff, B. & Cavaney, J. (2011). Risk: A very short introduction. Oxford University Press.
- Hill, L. A., Tabards, E. & Swan, T. (2021). Drive innovation with better decision- making. Harvard Business Review, November- December 2021, pp. 70-79.
- Liekerman, A. (2020). The elements of good judgment: How to improve your decision- making. Harvard Business Review, January- February 2020, pp. 103-111.
- Lovelle, D., Koller, T., Uline, R. & Kahneman, D. (2020). Your company is too risk averse. Harvard Business Review, March- April 2020, pp. 104- 111
- Martin, R. L. & Golsby-Smith, T. (2017). Management is much more than a science: The limits of

data-driven decision making. Harvard Business Review, September- October 2017, pp. 129-135.
- Miller, C.C. & Ireland, R. D. (2005). Intuition in strategic decision making: Friend or foe in the fast-paced 21St century. Academy of Management Executive, 2005, Vol. 19, No. 1, pp. 19-30.

# 5 ECONOMICS

## 5.1 ECONOMICS SCOPE

Economics is the discipline that studies the production, distribution, and consumption of goods and services.

The fundamental fact that dominates all economic activity is the limitation of available resources and, therefore, the scarcity of economic goods. Economics studies how society allocates limited resources to meet people's needs. The fundamental problems of economics are:

- What to produce?
- How much to produce?
- How to produce it?
- For whom to produce?

## 5.2 ECONOMIC SYSTEMS

The main economic systems are:

- **Capitalism or market system**. It is the economic system in which people own all or most of the means of production and distribution and they produce profits for their owners.

- **Socialism**. It is the economic system in which the State owns all or most of the means of production and distribution and they generate well-being for the community.

Capitalism has been imposing itself on the world, as it has shown greater capacity to generate wealth and, at the same time, allows greater freedom to people. However, capitalism has led to enormous inequality in the distribution of wealth, which has led to seeking a third way or intermediate path between capitalism and socialism. In any case, the reality is that almost no country is entirely capitalist or entirely socialist; for example, in many capitalist countries, especially in Europe, there are important State-owned enterprises and/or extensive social security or welfare systems for the community and, on the other hand, socialist countries, including Russia and China, have allowed private companies, both domestic and foreign, to operate in various sectors of their economies.

## 5.3  MICROECONOMICS

Microeconomics is the study of the economic activities of individuals and companies.

## 5.3.1 Factors of production

The usual factors of production are land, labor, and capital. Each factor of production requires a reward: land, rent; labor, wages; and capital, interest. Knowledge is a new factor of production and is becoming the most important.

## 5.3.2 Analysis of demand and supply

Demand and supply analysis is concerned with determining the quantities of products to sell at different prices. With a few exceptions, the higher the price, the lower the quantity demanded and vice versa. Markets reach equilibrium at the price at which supply (quantity supplied) equals demand (quantity demanded).

The price elasticity of demand is the percentage change in the quantities demanded determined by a given percentage change in price. If consumers are sensitive to price changes, for example by buying more units if prices fall, their demand is elastic. On the other hand, if they are not sensitive to these changes, since they buy the same number of units even if prices vary, their demand is inelastic.

## 5.3.3 The break-even point analysis

Break-even analysis determines the sales volume at

which a company can cover all its costs without making or losing money. Break-even analysis involves determining the firm's fixed costs and variable costs required to produce a given volume of sales. Profits only occur if sales exceed the sales volume corresponding to the break-even point (point at which revenue is equal to the total costs of the company).

### 5.3.4 Opportunity cost and marginal cost

Increasing the production of a good or service requires incurring a cost or sacrifice; economists call these costs opportunity costs, because they represent costs not used to take advantage of other investment opportunities. Two concepts closely related to opportunity cost are marginal income and marginal cost; that is, the aggregate income and cost, respectively, because of producing and selling an additional unit.

### 5.3.5 Utility and marginal utility

Utility is the ability of a good or service to satisfy a need. Marginal utility of a good is the increase in total utility provided by the consumption of an additional unit of that good.

### 5.3.6 The forms of the market

Perfect competition is based on the existence of small competing companies, with no predominant influence of any of them in control of the market. However, markets do not work ideally in the world and perfect competition is virtually non-existent.

Imperfect competition, which prevails, occurs when one or a few firms control the market. If a single selling company controls the market, it is a monopoly; if a single purchasing company controls it, it is a monopsony. If few selling companies control the market, it is an oligopoly; if a few purchasing companies control it, it is an oligopsony.

## 5.4 MACROECONOMICS

Macroeconomics is the study of the economy as a whole. It focuses on the aggregate changes in the economy such as unemployment, growth rate, gross domestic product, and inflation.

### 5.4.1 National income

National income is the value of goods and services produced in a country in each period. The gross domestic product (GDP) is equivalent to national income, measured as the sum of consumption, investment, and public expenditure. Gross domestic product and its growth rate are usually the basic indicators of the functioning of a country's economy, although they do not measure, of course, the quality of life of its inhabitants.

### 5.4.2 Economic development

An underdeveloped nation is one whose real per capita income is low relative to per capita income in more developed nations. The key to development lies in four fundamental factors: population, natural resources, capital formation, and technology.

To develop, a nation must:

- Improve the education and health of its human resources.
- Make better use of available natural resources.
- Correct inequalities in the distribution of wealth and accumulate capital through saving.
- Stimulate innovation or technological imitation.

In addition, economic development requires strengthening institutions (bureaucratic quality, judicial efficiency, microcredits) and promote democracy, civil liberties, and civic participation.

Inequalities in economic development between rich and poor countries have been on the rise over the past two hundred years, especially since World War

II, and there is little indication that the poor world can catch up with the rich in the immediate future. The best thing the rich world can do for the poor is to offer technical and financial aid to support the local businesses – including educational and primary care – that people are willing to create.

The United Nations Development Program (UNDP) has sought to replace or improve the concept of economic development by orienting it towards human development, defined as "the process of expanding the capacities of people who expand their options and opportunities." There is an index of human development, proposed by economist Amartya Sen, which considers life expectancy, education, and per capita income.

### 5.4.3    Public expenditure

The economic functions of the State have been continuously expanding in all countries, with public spending increasing faster than national income. There are two ways to reduce public spending:

- Increasing the efficiency of public administration.
- Restricting the functions of the State.

### 5.4.4    Taxes

Taxes give the State the resources it needs to

conduct its activities. The two main criteria governing modern tax systems are:

- Tax Individuals according to the advantages or benefits that each may receive from the activity of the State.
- Tax individuals in such a way as to achieve the redistribution of income that society considers fair.

### 5.4.5 Money

Money is any means we can use to purchase goods or services (cash, checks, bonds). The supply or sum of money in a country is equal to: All cash in the hands of the public and all checking accounts (M1) + All savings accounts (M2).

A higher speed of circulation of money causes an increase in the demand for goods and services (in terms of money), which in turn leads to an increase in prices. On the contrary, a slower speed of circulation of money causes a decrease in the demand for goods and services, which in turn leads to a decrease in prices.

### 5.4.6 Aggregate supply and aggregate demand

Aggregate supply is the total capacity of a nation to produce goods and services. Aggregate demand is all the money that people, businesses, and government spend on goods and services. Aggregate supply equals aggregate demand at an equilibrium price and production level.

### 5.4.7 Inflation and unemployment

The causes and effects of the general rise in prices and wages (inflation) and unemployment are one of the most important problems studied by economics. If aggregate demand grows faster than aggregate supply, the overall price level rises; that is, inflation occurs. Conversely, if aggregate demand is below aggregate supply, unemployment occurs.

Monetary policy and fiscal policy are the two basic ways to balance aggregate demand and aggregate supply, to prevent both inflation and unemployment. Monetary policy is the regulation of the volume of money in circulation and interest rates, and fiscal policy is the regulation of taxes and public spending. Unfortunately, preventing one of those problems usually leads to the other. Reducing monetary liquidity, raising interest rates, decreasing public spending, and raising taxes, corrects inflation, but all these measures could cause economic recession and increase unemployment.

## 5.4.8 Government intervention in the economy

Keynesian economists, i.e., supporters of John Maynard Keynes (1883-1946), argue that government intervention, for example by increasing public spending, can significantly improve the functioning of the economy. By contrast, monetarists, supporters of Milton Friedman (1912-2006), believe that markets work best if left alone, with minimal government intervention limited to controlling the availability of money.

## 5.4.9 The roles of the Central Bank

The Central Bank (called the Federal Reserve in the US) is usually responsible for a country's monetary policy. The Central Bank can play many roles, including:

- Regulator of the amount of money in circulation.
- Government banker.
- Lender to commercial banks.
- Issuer of coins and banknotes.

The Central Bank or Federal Reserve has three monetary tools at its disposal to regulate the economy:

- Changing the discount rate (the rate at which you lend money to banks).

- Buying or selling government securities or treasuries.
- Changing the reserve requirements of financial institutions (percentage that banks must keep with respect to the money deposited in them by their customers).

### 5.4.10 The exchange rate

Buying and selling abroad presupposes an exchange rate between domestic and foreign currency. Supply and demand set free exchange rates daily; however, governments can intervene to establish a fixed exchange rate. The devaluation of a country's currency, so that it decreases in value with respect to foreign ones, usually raises its exports and decreases its imports. Overvaluation usually has the opposite effect.

### 5.4.11 The balance of payments

A country's international balance of payments refers to the transactions that consume or provide its foreign currency and relates its total exports of goods and services to its total imports. The devaluation of a country's currency, by raising its exports and decreasing its imports, may be necessary to correct serious balance-of-payments difficulties.

## 5.4.12 The regulation of the international economy

The International Monetary Fund, the World Bank, international cooperation programs and free trade agreements are important for streamlining international trade and avoiding undesirable imbalances:

- **The International Monetary Fund (IMF)** has a regulatory role for international monetary behavior and a credit function aimed at providing financial assistance to member countries to solve balance-of-payments problems.
- **The World Bank** is one of the most important sources of financing and knowledge for developing countries, with the aim of ending extreme poverty and promoting shared prosperity.
- **The World Trade Organization (WTO)** is the only international organization that deals with the rules governing trade between countries.

## 5.5 RECOMMENDED READING

- Dasgupta, P. (2007). Economics: A very short introduction. Oxford University Press.
- Dixit, A. (2014). Microeconomics: A very short introduction. Oxford University Press.

- Friedman, M. (2020). Capitalism and Freedom. University of Chicago Press.
- Keynes, J.M. (2016) General theory of occupation, interest, and money. Harcourt, Brace & World.
- Larrain B., F. (2020). Macroeconomics. The MIT Press.
- Mankiw, N. G., Taylor, M. P., and Ashwin, A. (2017). Business Economics. Cengage Learning.
- Marx, K. (2018). Capital Vol. 1, 2 & 3. Independently published.
- Sen, A. (2000). Development as freedom. Anchor
- Smith, A. (2003). The wealth of nations. Bantam Classics.

# 6 ETHICS AND CORPORATE SOCIAL RESPONSIBILITY

## 6.1 ETHICS

Managers should behave ethically. Ethics, a distinction between good and evil, is not so much a matter of philosophy or something regulated by policies, norms, or codes. It is simply a matter of personal conviction.

### 6.1.1 Ethical problems in business

We observe daily all kinds of unvirtuous actions in the business world:

- Bribes.
- Fraud.
- Exploitation and harsh treatment of employees.
- Extortion to suppliers.
- Tax evasion.
- Non-compliance with laws.
- Environmental damage.
- Social irresponsibility.

These actions are committed by normal people, whom probably no one (including themselves) suspected of such ethical faults when they were students or young professionals. For this reason, no one should consider himself exempt from falling into these vices when entering the business environment.

Many managers try to justify their wrongdoing by arguing that:

- Ethics is relative and depends on circumstances.
- The business world is exceedingly difficult and leaves them no choice.
- Everything is valid to be successful.
- They must do the same as their competitors do.

But those arguments are just excuses to hide their incompetence, ambition, and lack of attachment to principles and values.

### 6.1.2  Ethics codes and committees

Some companies establish ethics codes, programs, and committees to try to ensure correct behavior by members of the organization. However, codes of ethics are often only means of protecting themselves from the wrongdoing of their employees and ethics programs are only apparent instruments to improve the image of the company and ensure a good reputation. In any case, ethics codes and committees are useless if people do not give importance to acting with dignity and honesty when they hold a position in a company, especially positions of greater responsibility.

### 6.1.3 The example of senior executives

Integrity must be a top executive priority so people can take it seriously across the company. The most important thing to ensure good ethical behavior in the company is clear example and messages sent from senior management to ensure:

- **The practice of lawful business.** Respect for integrity in relations with the fundamental actors of the company (customers, suppliers, partners, investors, and employees)
- **Corporate social responsibility.** The ethical conduct of managers has a positive impact on corporate culture and employee motivation and adds an integrative and orderly aspect to the management of the company. It is a motivating factor for teamwork, an ally for the improvement of productivity, a factor of individual growth, an additional element of legal protection that results in greater legal certainty, legitimizes managerial actions, and is a fundamental element of the good public image of the company.

Being ethical in the company is not easy. Therefore, it is important that its managers strive to develop their capacities to make decisions that are efficient at the economic level, acceptable at the social and psychological level and ethical. Managers should discard the use of intuition when it comes to managing ethical issues and do so in an orderly manner, comparing available options, making decisions that create more value for all parties, and setting aside the potential effects of decisions on themselves.

Managers should also contribute to creating an organization that helps employees behave more honorably by providing them with training in experiences with ethical dilemmas, fostering psychological safety when minor failures occur, conducting pre- and post-evaluations of initiatives with ethical components, and creating a culture of service by encouraging volunteer work and ethical mentoring.

### 6.1.4 The importance of ethics for companies

We live in a globalized world, with frequent crises of all kinds that spread rapidly throughout the world, and in this context ethics and social responsibility are even more necessary. People suffer crises and are rightly upset when they see that these crises are due, to a considerable extent, to ethical and corporate social responsibility failures, often in complicity with government officials. Companies that act with ethics and social responsibility differentiate from those that do not act in that way and become worthy of the trust of the people.

A good company, an excellent company, must be an ethical company. An ethical company will always look at the consequences of its decisions on all the people involved: the managers themselves, employees, customers and suppliers, the local community, society, and even future generations (the environmental dimension). The ethics of companies must always be an ethic of responsibility, considering the consequences of their decisions and actions.

Most companies define success in monetary terms, but the reality is that the most important thing is values (respect, responsibility, transparency, honesty, compliance). Companies that practice their core values satisfy all those interested in it (customers, shareholders, employees, suppliers, distributors, regulators). Values come first, before strategy, products, finance, or business plans, and are what determine the true success of companies.

## 6.2 CORPORATE SOCIAL RESPONSIBILITY

### 6.2.1 The meaning and scope of corporate social responsibility

Corporate social responsibility refers to the ways in

which companies manage their relationship with society.

Companies make profits from society and should give something back to society. This is the foundation of corporate social responsibility and is based on company ethics; that is, in their concern for the consequences of their decisions on all people.
Therefore, ethics and social responsibility are two intimately related concepts.

In times of globalization and crisis, companies assuming responsibility is a demand for justice. In addition, corporate social responsibility generates the social cohesion that is essential for the economy to function well.

Corporate social responsibility is not only philanthropic actions or selfless help to others, since it is more important the concern for the social impacts of business operations, including:

- Effects on human health and safety.
- Respect and promotion of diversity.
- Policies of equal opportunities.
- Environmental impacts.
- Consumption of scarce resources.
- Impacts occurring in international supply chains (e.g., working conditions in agricultural, textile and footwear industries in developing countries).

- Downstream effects and responsibility of companies in the use and disposal of their products.

Although many companies have become aware of their social responsibility, many others distort their action in this field by simply orienting it to promote a good corporate image and avoid criticism from stakeholders. However, social responsibility should not be a propaganda activity of companies but a true activity of public service and good corporate citizenship.

### 6.2.2 Measuring corporate social responsibility

Although difficult, there are some methods of measuring corporate social responsibility. Many of the indicators used refer to the results of operations (for example, investments, hours of voluntary work of employees, and number of people benefited); however, these indicators do not answer questions about the difference that social responsibility activities make in solving the problems considered and in the sustainability of the planet.

### 6.3 RECOMMENDED READING

- Bazerman, M. H. (2020). A new model for ethical leadership. Harvard Business Review, September-October 2020, pp. 91-97.

- Chesnut, R. (2021). Why building an ethical culture must start at the top? Interview conducted by Ally Mac Donald. Sloan Management Review, Vol. 63 (1).
- Johnson, C. E. (2021). Organizational ethics: A practical approach. SAGE Publications, Inc.
- Moon, J. (2014). Corporate social responsibility: A very short introduction. Oxford University Press.
- Polman, P. & Winston, A. (2021). The net positive manifesto. Harvard Business Review, September-October 2021, pp. 124-131.
- Smith, I. H. and Kochari, M. (2021). Building an ethical company. Harvard Business Review, November- December 2021, pp. 132-139.

# 7 FINANCE

## 7.1 THE FINANCE FUNCTION

The operation of companies is strongly associated with their money flows. Companies need money to be able to conduct their activities and they generate money because of the sale of their goods or services. The acquisition of funds to meet current and future needs and the management of money in the company to maximize its profitability constitute the function of finance management.

## 7.2 FINANCE MANAGEMENT

The financial managers of the company must answer questions such as these:
- How do we finance ourselves?
- How do we manage cash?
- How should we compensate our shareholders?
- How should we communicate information to our shareholders and lenders?
- How should we analyze our investment opportunities?
- How much is the company worth?

## 7.2.1 Financing

The goal of finance management is to raise enough capital at the lowest possible cost for the level of risk the company is willing to live with.

Companies capture the resources required for their incorporation and operations in several diverse ways. They can use their own capital, resort to external financing to obtain loans or credits, deduct bills of exchange or other documents of this kind in their possession, and can also issue shares and bonds.

In general, regular working capital should come from long-term sources (stocks and/or long-term liabilities), while fluctuating working capital needs typically require short-term financing. In the case of acquiring obligations, is convenient to match the maturity of the obligation with the period in which the financed asset produces income.

The optimal capital structure is the combination of own and external resources that maximizes the value of the company; that is, it defines that indebtedness would be reasonable to achieve a higher valuation. In general, the more debt you have is better, if the indebtedness does not put at risk the solvency and stability of the company.

### 7.2.2 Cash handling

Cash management assumes a balance between the need to have enough cash for the operation of the company, always, and the convenience of earning maximum interest by investing the available cash. Cash availability should depend on forecasted cash flows, the likelihood of running out of cash, debt conditions, and the ability to borrow.

### 7.2.3 Shareholder relations

The success of finance management includes maintaining appropriate relationships with the investment community. Dividend decisions and financial reports are the visible elements of this relationship. The dividends or profits that companies distribute among their shareholders must be determined in accordance with legal restrictions, the financial needs of companies, and the expectations of shareholders.

### 7.2.4 Investment decisions

In addition to investing in its own growth (acquisition of other companies, construction of new plants, research and development of new products, technological development, organizational change) or in partnerships with other companies to undertake new businesses, companies can invest in the stock markets (stocks, bonds, options, futures) the money they do not require in their cash flow.

Several approaches can be useful in evaluating a company's investment opportunities. The task in all approaches is to find the difference between the net benefits accrued from each alternative and the financial burden incurred to achieve the benefits. The basic principle of all of them is the variation of the value of money over time.

There are four methods for the evaluation of investment alternatives:

- Recovery period (time to recover the investment).
- Net present value (present value of net cash earnings, discounted at the rate of the company's cost of capital or cost-weighted rate, calculated on the combined capital structure).
- Internal rate of return (discount rate for which the net present value of an investment is equal to zero).
- Return on investment (ratio of income generated and cost savings between the investment made, expressed in percentage terms).

The evaluation of investment alternatives should consider not only the expected benefits but the risk that each investment opportunity entails. As a rule, the greater the risk associated with an investment opportunity, the greater the profit expected by the investor.

Investment decisions need more than a single financial projection. Managers must analyze how sensitive the estimated results are to variations in the assumptions on which the forecasts have been based. The best projects are the ones that make sense even when the future turns out worse than anticipated.

Simulation techniques, considering probability distributions of sales volume, sales prices, market growth rate, market share, required investment, operational costs, and fixed costs, among other variables, can be useful in evaluating risky investments.

### 7.2.5 The value of the company

The value of the company is the price that a company has for all those interested in it (financial creditors and shareholders). The value of a company can be determined from the accounting point of view (equity or capital of the company) if it is to liquidate and close the company, distributing the net worth among the shareholders or owners, but it must be estimated as the present value of all its future cash flows if it is to buy a company and determine the profit that can be obtained from it.

## 7.3 ACCOUNTING

Every business operates on financial data. To make the necessary decisions in the management of the money of any type of company. The financial managers must have accounting information. Accounting is the order adopted to keep the accounts of the company. The purpose of accounting is to present the financial condition of a company so that interested parties can make their assessments. There are three financial statements for that purpose:

- **The balance sheet:** A representation of the financial situation of the company at a given date, showing the amount of assets, liabilities, and capital or net worth. Assets are all the physical resources that a company can put to work in the service of the business, liabilities are debts to suppliers and other creditors, and capital or net worth is the difference between assets and liabilities (this is the fundamental law or equation of accounting: capital = assets − liabilities). The data contained in the balance sheet is useful especially when compared with the same information from one or more years.
- **The income statement or profit and loss statement:** Shows the financial results in a given

period, usually one year, indicating the income, expenses, and the resulting gain or loss in that period. Of the three financial statements, the income statement is the most important for the work of a manager.

- **The cash flow statement:** Shows the evolution and/or estimates of income and expenses in the coming months or year, indicating the availability or deficiency of cash throughout that period.

## 7.4 FINANCIAL ANALYSIS

Accounting information allows the financial analysis of the company. Financial analysis includes the analysis of the company's funding needs, its financial performance and condition, and its business risks. By analyzing these factors, the company can determine its financial needs and negotiate with external capital providers.

The analysis of financial statements consists of the evaluation of the current state of a company by calculating indicators, ratios, or measures in four areas of financial performance, then comparing them with the indicators of other similar companies:

- **Liquidity** (the company's ability to meet its short-term obligations): current ratio or liquidity ratio

(current assets/current liabilities), acid or rapid test or cash ratio.
- **Indebtedness or leverage** (level of indebtedness of the company): total indebtedness or debt-to-equity ratio, short-term indebtedness, long-term indebtedness, interest coverage.
- **Profitability** (degree of success in reaching the desired levels of profit): return on assets, return on equity, return on sales, profit margin or gross profit, profit before interest and taxes.
- **Efficiency or exploitation** (effectiveness of the use of resources): rotation of assets (sales/total assets), period or average term of collection, period, or average term of payment to suppliers, days of inventory.

Other parameters for assessing a company's financial health include:

- Value of the company.
- Earnings per share (price/earnings ratio of shares).
- Growth in sales or profit.
- Economic value added (EVA) or difference between the company's net income (before taxes) and its cost of capital.

- Measures of productivity (sales per employee or net income per employee).

## 7.5  THE BUDGET

The budget is the advanced calculation of the expenses and income of the company foreseen for a certain period, usually the next year.

The budget must be ambitious, but realistic. To elaborate it, it must be based on the desired goals in the period (for example, increase in sales, reduction of administrative expenses, or reduction of inventories). Then it must be determined how to achieve these goals (increase in personnel, necessary resources, development of new products, elimination of products, increase or reduction of prices, incursion into new markets).

Budget control is the process of comparing the results with the budget to verify achievements or remedy differences.

## 7.6  RECOMMENDED READING

- Ashar, K. (2019). Financial management: Essentials you always wanted to know. Vibrant Publishers.

- Desai, M. (2019). How finance works: The HBR guide to thinking smart about the numbers. Harvard Business Review Press.
- Ross, S.A., Westerfield, R. W., Jaffe, J., and Jordan, B.D. (2021). Corporate Finance. International edition, McGraw- Hill.

# 8 HUMAN RESOURCES

## 8.1 HUMAN RESOURCES

Organizations need employees for their existence and operation, called personnel, human resources, people, or human capital. The use of the term "human resources" seems a mistake. Equating people and the work they do in companies with resources or factors of production, such as capital or land, has connotations offensive to human dignity. Unfortunately, however, this is not a mistake. This is exactly how companies look at their people. Despite abundant corporate rhetoric about the importance of people and equally abundant research demonstrating the desirability of treating employees with respect and involving them in decisions, the reality is that many companies see people as a disposable resource and fire them if they do not achieve the expected results, usually arbitrarily established by incompetent managers.

Although all managers say that their most important asset is their employees and that the success of the companies depends on them, the reality is that there is a large gap between what they say and what they do in relation to human resources management. The truth is that most managers privilege economic results over the well-being of their people and treat employees as disposable resources, evaluating them according to automatic criteria and replacing them with contracted or independent workers or lower-cost employees.

## 8.2 HUMAN RESOURCES MANAGEMENT

Human resources management is the function of attracting, directing, developing, and retaining the people that the company needs to achieve its objectives and goals. The responsibility for this function corresponds to all the managers of the company, who can rely on the human resources department or unit.

### 8.2.1 The human resources management process

The human resources management process comprises the following core activities:

**Planning.** It serves to ensure that the company has, on a consistent and appropriate basis, the required staff.

**Recruitment.** It develops a series of job candidates, according to the human resources plan. The purpose of recruitment is to form a pool of candidates large enough for managers to choose the qualified employees they need. In general, companies should try to recruit candidates more for their potential than for their experience and should try to improve the perceptions that these candidates have of them, to become more attractive, especially for the most talented candidates.

**Selection.** It involves using applications, resumes, interviews, job and skills tests, as well as reference checks, to evaluate, select, and present candidates to the managers, who will choose from them. In general, the selection process must determine whether the candidate possesses the appropriate competencies to conduct the type of work required and whether they possess the ability to adapt well to the culture of the organization.

**Induction.** It is the process of orientation to the new employee, which serves to help the hired people adapt to the organization without difficulty.

**Training and development.** They seek to increase the capabilities of employees, to increase the effectiveness of the organization. Training programs maintain or improve performance in present work, while development programs aim to develop capabilities for future positions.

**Performance evaluation.** It compares the person's job performance with the parameters or objectives established for that person's position and allows to determine their variable remuneration.

**Compensation.** Compensation or remuneration systems should attract and retain the most talented people and stimulate them to perform the best possible. In addition to wage compensation, companies may offer other types of benefits and services to their employees to improve their quality of life and satisfaction within the company. The necessary people must be well paid and must feel that the compensation system is fair. Executive compensation particularly must align with corporate strategy to drive better performance.

**Career planning.** It serves to guide the development of people within the company, according to their value to the organization.

### 8.2.2 Employee experience

Employee experience is the process of working in a company and feeling, facing, and encountering problems or satisfactions during the time of employment. Employees do not only value what the company gives to them but also how they feel about the company.

Star performers need to feel special. Good compensation is not the solution. To retain their unique talent companies should listen to their ideas, support their growth and development, and show appreciation to them as often as possible.

### 8.2.3 Human resources policies

Human resources policies are the principles or objectives established by a company as a guide to the management of its relationships with employees. Policies at each stage of the human resource management process are the starting point for all administrative relationships with employees.

### 8.2.4 Industrial relations

Labor relations include the administration and monitoring of compliance with the policies and standards established by the laws and by the company itself and the resolution of conflicts that may arise between the company and its workers due to non-compliance with these provisions, the existence of an inadequate organizational climate or the aspiration for greater benefits.

Most conflicts between a company and its workers have their origin in:

- Lack of communication.
- Failure to comply with collective agreements.
- The existence of an inadequate organizational climate.

Therefore, the company must ensure that it maintains adequate systems and channels of communication with all its workers and with the unions that can represent them, monitor compliance with collective agreements and ensure that it continuously evaluates and improves the organizational climate.

## 8.3 LABOR LEGISLATION

Labor legislation is the set of laws and regulations that aim to regulate work activities, both regarding the rights of the worker, as well as his obligations and the same for the employer. Labor laws exist in all countries, albeit with some differences, and the International Labor Organization (ILO), a United Nations agency, seeks to set standards, formulate policies, and develop programs that promote decent work for all, improve social protection and strengthen dialogue in addressing work-related issues around the world.

In the United States, the main labor laws are as follows:

- **The National Labor Relations Act of 1935 (NLRA)**, which encourages collective bargaining by protecting workers' full freedom of association.
- **The Fair Labor Standards Act of 1938 (FLSA)** sets standards for minimum wage, overtime pay, hour and pay accounting, and enforcing standards for

the employment of minors. These standards apply to full-time and part-time workers, employees in the private sector, the federal government, and state and local governments.
- **The Taft-Hartley Act of 1947** (also called the "Labor Relations Management Act") established several new limitations on guilds or unions, removing several restrictions on employers set forth in the National Labor Relations Act.
- **Anti-Discrimination Laws** (Civil Rights Act, 1964; Age Discrimination in Employment Act, 1967; Americans with Disabilities Act, 1990), which protect against discrimination at work based on race or color, sex, pregnancy, sexual harassment, age, or disability.
- **The Occupational Safety and Health Act of 1970**, enacted to prevent workers injuries or death on the job. The law requires employers to provide their employees with working conditions free of known hazards. The law created the Occupational Safety and Health Administration (OSHA), which is responsible for ensuring compliance.

## 8.4 THE DIVERSITY OF THE WORKFORCE

As a result of globalization, the international expansion of companies and the migration of workers are making the workforce in companies increasingly diverse. In the same way, the increasing participation of women and changing attitudes towards people with different sexual orientations are also significantly changing the composition of staff in companies.

Effectively managing that diversity and taking advantage of differences to enrich decision-making and innovation processes is a major challenge for both human resources departments and all company managers.

There is no empirical evidence that simply diversifying the workforce makes a company more profitable; however, companies can benefit from diversity if their leaders create a psychologically safe work environment, combat systems of discrimination and subordination, accept the styles of employees from different identity groups, and make cultural differences a resource for learning and improving the workforce. organizational effectiveness.

## 8.5 SAFETY AND HEALTH IN THE WORK ENVIRONMENT

International conventions and the laws of many countries require the establishment of basic occupational health services, defined as preventive services, including counselling to the worker on the requirements necessary to establish and maintain a safe and healthy working environment, which favors optimal physical and mental health in relation to work and the adaptation of the latter to the capacities of the workers, considering their state of physical and mental health.

A health problem that demands special attention is that of stress at work. Stress is the physical or mental alteration of an individual by subjecting their organism to overwork and nervous tension. Employees of many companies live under many pressures and demands and in some cases must work too many hours a week. Stress manifests itself in several ways, usually in the form of physiological, psychological, or behavioral changes. Moderate stress stimulates the body and increases its ability to react, but too much stress imposes restrictions or unattainable demands on people, whose performance, as a result, falls. In addition to decreasing their productivity, people can get sick as a cause of stress. Some people manage to cope better with stress; however, the important thing is that companies become aware of this problem and moderate their demands.

## 8.6 REMOTE WORK

Technology and events such as the pandemic generated by Covid-19 have demonstrated the opportunities of remote work. Many jobs still require the physical presence of workers, especially in construction, factories, direct customer service companies such as barbershops and beauty salons, transport companies, schools for children and adolescents, gyms, hospitals, hotels, restaurants, and security services. However, in many other jobs employees can work from home, with advantages for them and savings of physical space and operating expenses for companies. Companies should trust employees and not assume that if they are not in the office, they are not productive.

In some cases, it may be convenient to combine both modalities in a hybrid way, taking advantage of the short-term advantages of remote work without harming the long-term performance of the company; offices can then serve as places to renew social ties, build trust, and facilitate learning and innovation. Social capital, that is, the set of resources derived from the networks of institutionalized relationships between managers and employees of the company, based on trust, cooperation, and acceptance of certain norms, is critical for the future of hybrid work.

## 8.7 RECOMMENDED READING

- Cappelli, P. (2020). Stop overengineering people management. Harvard Business Review, September- October 2020, pp. 56-63.
- Deal, J. J. & Levenson, A. (2021). Figuring out social capital is critical for the future of hybrid work. Sloan Management Review, Vol. 63 (1).
- Ely, R.J. & Thomas, D.A. (2020). Getting serious about diversity. Harvard Business Review, November- December 2020, pp. 115-122.
- Fayard, A.L., Weeks, J. and Kahn, M. (2021). Designing the hybrid office. Harvard Business Review, March- April 2021, pp. 114-123.
- Gartner (2022). Rethinking your approach to employee experience. Harvard Business Review, March- April 2022, pp. 17-21.
- Gilbert, J. (2020). Human resource management: Essentials you always wanted to know. Vibrant Publishers.
- Groysberg, B., Abbot, S., Marino, M.R. & Aksoy, M. (2021). Compensation packages that actually

- drive performance. Harvard Business Review, January- February 2021, pp. 102-111.
- Martin, R. L. (2022). The real secret to retaining talent. Harvard Business Review, March- April 2022, pp. 127-133.
- Pfeffer, J. (2007). What were they thinking? Unconventional wisdom about management. Harvard Business Review Press.
- Westerman, G. (2021). Rethinking assumptions about how employees work. Sloan Management Review, Fall 2021, Vol. 63 (1).

# 9 INTERNATIONAL BUSINESS

## 9.1 INTERNATIONALIZATION

Companies that want to grow, as part of their strategy, should consider internationalization; that is, to market their products or operate in other countries.

### 9.1.1 Benefits and opportunities of internationalization

Although the international expansion of their operations seems a challenging task for some companies, the benefits and opportunities associated with that expansion are many. There are not only business opportunities, but opportunities to improve their quality and efficiency and enormous potential to discover and implement innovations. International expansion reduces costs because increasing volume results in economies of scale. The presence in more demanding markets helps a company to improve the quality of its products. Global market activity can increase the preference of global customers because of their global availability, service, and recognition. A global strategy approach increases competitive effectiveness.

## 9.1.2 Risks of internationalization

However, despite its many benefits, the expansion of geographical space across borders is likely to increase coordination costs and generate trade, transport, and tariff barrier costs; on the other hand, it is possible that a loss of concentration in the client occurs, due to the need to serve a very wide and diverse base of customers. Additionally, although the globalized business environment provides many opportunities, it is less protected and carries many more risks, which requires a more detailed analysis of the political, legal, economic, social, and cultural environment of all the countries in which to develop activities.

## 9.1.3 The selection of countries in which to conduct operations

In general, companies should not venture into countries with low business growth potential if they do not have special competitive advantages. If you have these advantages, you must make the most of these markets to generate and provide funds that allow you to venture into countries with high potential for business growth, where there may be greater risks. Different countries can play different strategic roles as part of a total overall strategy.

Although it is a company's competitiveness that will determine its success in international markets, companies can benefit from defining their strategies by taking advantage of the competitive advantages of the nations in which they operate. The competitiveness of a nation, in each industry or sector of economic activity, requires:

- Appropriate conditions of company strategy and industry structure.
- Significant rivalry or internal competition.
- Ease of access to the necessary raw materials and availability of skilled labor, infrastructure, and technology.
- Significant local demand and consumer expectations.
- The presence of adequate related industries and support to the industry or sector of economic activity in question.

### 9.1.4   Options for trading in each country

Companies usually start their activities in a foreign country by exporting their products or services to that country, with the support of a local representative. However, many consider it necessary to have a foreign direct investment (FDI) or direct presence in the country, for which they can constitute an affiliate or subsidiary, acquire a local company, grant a franchise or a combination of these strategies. They must also decide whether to manufacture their products in that country or import it from some other country in which they build their plants or factories.

In general, multinational companies, which conduct operations and have a direct presence in several countries, arise when:

- They find localization advantages to operate in several countries.
- They have their own resources and capabilities that allow them to compete favorably with local or foreign companies operating in those countries.
- They want to internalize their operations; that is, avoid the costs of operating through an intermediary

Decisions on the form of penetration in each country depend on the analysis of all factors related to the decision (legal, economic, commercial, political, social). Some can go very quickly in that process, but in general manufacturing companies usually take longer than marketing or service companies.

A multinational company is global when it operates worldwide or at least in the main markets: the

United States, Europe, and China.

## 9.1.5 The importance of information

International expansion is based on information. Knowing how to act in the global market is what allows a company to succeed in this strategy. Companies need information to:

- Break with the mental schemes used to in their local market.
- Build the capacity at your headquarters to oversee international business.
- Invest in the development of managerial skills in its units abroad.
- Compare themselves to the best, learn from them, and have the confidence to confront and challenge them.

## 9.1.6 The challenges of global companies

Globalization imposes great challenges on the managers of all companies, particularly those of multinationals. Managers of these companies need to understand the complexities of global business, conceive, and execute global strategies, and develop the new analytical approaches and organizational arrangements on which their competitive future rests.

In general, global companies achieve competitive advantages from their ability to transfer their expertise across borders and avoid mistakes.

While running any company is always a challenge, being a manager of a global company is usually a bigger challenge. Managers of global companies must:

- Understand and interpret local markets.
- Recognize opportunities and risks in different countries.
- Link activities and capabilities around the world.
- Build local resources and capacities.
- Transfer knowledge and experiences from one unit to another.
- Contribute to the development of a global strategy.
- Lead innovation efforts with universal application.

Several forces are complicating the geopolitical environment for multinational corporations, including growing global instability and frequent tensions between major world powers. Companies need, in this environment, to assess well their local, regional, and transnational risks and develop the diplomatic ability to operate internationally and ensure success in each country in which they operate.

Global companies with greater gender and race diversity are likely to be more innovative, achieve greater employee engagement, and outperform their competitors financially. To efficiently manage diversity, senior executives must lead by example, take charge of diversity initiatives, and foster diversity across the organization.

## 9.2　THE ORGANIZATION OF GLOBAL COMPANIES

A particular case of organizational design, and the most complex, is the organization of global companies. The organization of a global company involves designing the organization of the parent company, the organization of the regions, and the organization of the subsidiaries.

### 9.2.1　Affiliates and subsidiaries

In general, global companies need to establish organizational units or subsidiary companies in each of the countries in which they operate or at least in the most important of them, serving smaller countries from some medium or large neighboring country. These subsidiary companies could be national companies, dependencies of the global company, or divisions of the regional company, depending on what is most convenient from the taxes point of view.

The affiliate is a company controlled by the parent company, without the use of intermediaries, while the subsidiary is a company controlled through another company. There are also branches, which are not independent companies but are simply extensions of the parent company in another country.

### 9.2.2 Integration of operations

At its headquarters, global companies need to develop a global corporate vision and integrate the activities that the company conducts in the world. This organization should establish production where it is most convenient, and information and products should move efficiently between different regions and countries. It is necessary to promote cooperation and communication and eliminate any redundant effort or investment unless it is to maintain adequate flexibility in the business.

A key success factor for a global company is its ability to achieve the integration of its organization on a global scale. Integration depends on the ability to apply its fundamental technologies and share the knowledge acquired in all the countries or regions in which it operates. Integration includes products or technology but also all aspects of the business: market research, retail relations, customer service, and brand identity. A global strategy cannot succeed if there are barriers and resistance in the organization and if all aspects of the organization do not complement each other to support the desired global strategy.

### 9.2.3 Uniformity vs diversity

A frequent problem to solve in the organization of global companies and all large corporations, involves choosing between uniformity and diversity. Uniformity implies standardization and centrally administered procedures, with the purpose of ensuring greater efficiency in joint work; however, it involves greater bureaucracy (excessive complication and slowness in conducting operations, due to the existence of numerous rules and procedures that must be complied with to ensure uniformity). Diversity, on the other hand, means recognizing regional, market, product, technology, and goal differences, as well as leaving room for experimentation and innovation. Each company must choose the most appropriate balance between uniformity and diversity for its particular case, but it must always be careful to avoid bureaucracy or reduce it to the minimum possible.

### 9.2.4 Truly global companies

Although many companies are global simply because they operate around or most of the world, they are often not truly global, as their culture, mindset and customs are deeply rooted in the country of origin. To be truly global, companies need to adapt to the countries in which they operate, ensure that they have executives who have lived in many countries and know their customs and have effective communication systems that reduce the effects of distance and internal cultural differences.

## 9.3 THE INFLUENCE OF CULTURAL DIFFERENCES ON MANAGEMENT

As the second half of the twentieth century passed, the importance of international business grew, and companies and researchers realized that cultural differences required adjustments in the management of organizations in different countries. Geert Hofstede and then Fons Trompenaars and Charles Hampden-Turner, developed their theories or models of cultural dimensions, to describe and differentiate national cultures.

Cultural differences influence the way managers should relate to employees and run companies. In Latin America, for example, people give significant importance to relationships with others, they prefer to achieve results by working collectively, demand respectful treatment from managers, and question their decisions, while in the United States the individual effort is especially important, interpersonal relationships are less relevant, and many managers tend to give orders without discussion. Obviously, a Latin American manager can fail in the United States if he intends to relate to local employees and run a company as he would in his home country and, in the same way, an American manager can fail if he tries to transfer the usual practices in his country to the management of a company in Latin America. In general, the cultures of northern European countries more closely resemble American culture, and the cultures of European Mediterranean countries more closely resemble Latin American cultures. In China, on the other hand, culture is very collectivist, even more so than in Latin America, but also very authoritarian, even more so than in the United States.

The American dominance in the theory and practice of management, together with the significant importance of multinational companies with origin in that country, make management around the world very marked by the American model. However, these ideas must be adapted to local cultures.

## 9.4 THE FINANCE OF GLOBAL COMPANIES

In global companies, corporate finance management must answer not only traditional finance questions but questions like these:

- How should we finance our subsidiaries?
- How should we get money from our subsidiaries?
- How should we analyze the same investment opportunities in different countries?

The financing of international companies is complicated by the operation in different countries, which also generally have different regulations and economic systems. Although it is easier for international companies to acquire funds, being able to have very varied sources around the world, they must consider in their actions the different regulations that may exist for the remission of funds to and from each country. In addition, they must consider the fiscal and monetary policies of each country, to take advantage of favorable conditions and avoid unfavorable ones. The idea is to try to obtain not so much the best financial result in each country, but the best financial result for the international company.

## 9.5 RECOMMENDED READING

- Bartlett, C.A., and Ghoshal, S. (1992). What is a global manager? Harvard Business Review, August 2003, pp. 101-108.
- Czinkota, M. R., Ronkainen, I. A. and Gupta, S. (2021). International Business. Cambridge University Press, 9th edition.
- Desai, M. A. (2008). The finance function in a global corporation. Harvard Business Review, July- August 2008, pp. 108-112.
- Hendry, J. (2013). Management: A very short introduction. Oxford University Press.
- Steger, M. (2020). Globalization: A very short introduction. Oxford University Press, 5th edition.
- Trompenaars, F. & Hampden-Turner, C. (2020). Riding the waves of culture. McGraw-Hill Education, 4th edition.

# 10 LEADERSHIP

## 10.1 THE EVOLUTION OF THE CONCEPT OF LEADERSHIP

In the history of humanity there has always been an interest in leadership and for many centuries that interest referred only to the leader. Already in the second half of the twentieth century it became clear that in leadership not only leaders but also followers intervene and in the present century several researchers have highlighted, additionally, the influence of the context in the leadership process. We see then how from a single perspective, that of the leader, the concept of leadership has evolved to include the perspectives of the followers and the context:

"Leadership is a process that occurs when people, in a certain context, decide to follow a leader".

## 10.2 THE LEADER

Person-centered studies of the leader have addressed the leader's traits, styles, values, and competencies.

In the first half of the twentieth century, managers and researchers thought that leaders possess personality traits that differentiate them from non-leaders, but that was not true, according with research performed after World War II.

The interest of leadership studies moved then to the styles or modes of behavior of leaders, distinguishing, among others, the autocratic, democratic, and permissive styles (or "laissez faire"), and task-centered leadership or people-centered leadership, concluding that the best style depends on circumstances.

However, some authors considered that style is not the most important thing in a leader, but his personal qualities. For example, John Kotter, a professor at Harvard University, said, "The key is not in style. The key is in the substance. Is something that has to do with the basic way of working, not with appearances or tactics, but with that essence that changes little over time, no matter the difference of cultures, or industries ".

Then the research led to the values that a leader should possess, for example, courage or bravery, perseverance, respect, and integrity. Thus, the concepts of authentic leadership, ethical leadership, servant leadership, spiritual leadership, and responsible leadership emerged. Although all of these values are convenient and necessary, the reality is that very few leaders are truly virtuous, as Jeffrey Pfeffer, a professor at Stanford University, has stated: "Leaders are expected to be virtuous and responsible, so that members of the organization can trust them to protect them and care about their interests, but few leaders meet those requirements". This means that we should not idealize leaders too much.

On the other hand, throughout history many suitable competencies have been suggested for leaders (assertiveness, adaptability, communication, courage, creativity, empathy, diplomatic skills, emotional intelligence, persuasion, wisdom, sagacity, sense of humor, strategic vision, etc.); but reality shows that very few leaders have all these skills and not even most of them, although it is recognized that current leaders must possess the capacity to manage crises and cope with complexity, as well as think in an integrative or holistic way.

## 10.3 THE RELATIONSHIP BETWEEN THE LEADER AND THE FOLLOWERS

Difficulties in establishing common personal qualities in leaders led to more attention to the relationship between the leader and followers. By focusing on this relationship, the researchers recognized that the most important thing is not the personal qualities of the leaders but how followers perceive those qualities, since they are the ones who decide that someone is their leader. No matter how many personal competencies a person possesses, if he has no followers, he cannot be a leader.

It is often difficult to determine if the leader's actions led directly to the results or if these were the product of the interaction between leader and followers in each context. For these reasons, the focus shifted from "leader" to "leadership"; that is, to a social phenomenon rather than a person.

The leader, to sustain himself, must be able to influence their followers, but at the same time should accept their influence on him. If the followers perceive that the leader does not respond to their interests, they will withdraw their support and will cease to be their leader. In companies, the manager has a right to supervise and direct his subordinates, but that does not make him a leader. Leaders should not use their power only to control their followers but to support them and help them achieve the company's goals together. This need has given rise to the concept of shared leadership, also called distributed, collective, collaborative, or democratic. It is simply about trying to achieve results through people, collaborating with them rather than just giving them orders.

To be a leader, your subordinates should voluntarily agree to follow you, not because you are their boss but because they consider you a leader worthy of following. Of course, being a manager and a leader is better for itself and the organization. Their leadership ability should be greater as the manager occupies higher-level positions in a company. The main obstacle to greatness in many companies is ineffective leadership.

Among the studies and theories on the relationship between leaders and followers, the proposal, in the late 1970s, by James MacGregor Burns, historian, political scientist and biographer, has stood out. Burns identified two general types or models of relationship between leaders and followers, transactional leadership and transforming or transformational leadership:

- **Transactional leadership** is a process of exchange between leaders and followers.
- **Transformational leadership**, on the other hand, means the leader's ability to bring about significant changes in both followers and the organization.

Despite the differences between transactional leadership and transformational leadership, they are not two exclusive options but two different dimensions of leadership. A leader can simultaneously adopt transformational and transactional leadership behaviors.

Several authors argue that transformational

leadership is associated with the charisma or attractiveness of the leader's personality; although in general this is true, many charismatic leaders (for example, Hitler, Mao, and Fidel Castro, in the political sphere) manipulated their followers and led them to situations adverse to themselves.

## 10.4 THE IMPORTANCE OF CONTEXT

In the present century, several authors have argued that the relationship between the leader and the followers is a result of context; that is, the circumstances in which that relationship takes place. Context is now one of the three components of leadership, along with the leader and followers, and even that the three components have the same importance. Leadership is not a quality of a leader but the process that occurs when people agree to follow a leader in a certain context.

## 10.5 WOMEN'S PERFORMANCE AS LEADERS

Although women already hold half of the jobs in many countries, very few still actually hold leadership positions in companies. In many cultures, the prototype leader should have "masculine" characteristics (decisive, assertive, and independent), while the way women act (friendly, altruistic, concerned about taking care of others) is not perceived as suitable for a leadership role. These cultural prejudices make it difficult for women to rise to leadership positions in organizations. On the other hand, many women prefer to accept lower-ranking occupations and abandon the idea of ascending to leadership positions, to jointly meet the demands of work and family.

## 10.6 THE DEVELOPMENT OF NEW LEADERS

One of the main motivations of leadership studies has been to be able to formulate recommendations and establish procedures to develop new leaders.

Although there are many proposals to develop leaders within organizations, the task of becoming a leader seems to be a mostly individual endeavor. You learn to be a leader by acting like a leader, which means producing innovative ideas, making contributions outside of your area of expertise, and connecting people and resources toward a worthwhile goal.

Organizations can support those individual efforts by providing opportunities to those who demonstrate interest and leadership potential, so they can learn to lead other people and exert influence over them.

It is necessary to warn that all these recommendations assume that leaders can develop. Although most authors agree that leaders develop, they recognize that leaders must be born with certain personal qualities or develop them in their childhood and adolescence, long before they can be leaders in any field of activity. That is, not everyone can be a leader. Moreover, while possessing adequate skills is indispensable, this is not enough. For a person to become a leader, he needs a group that accepts him as such, at least in certain circumstances.

## 10.7 RECOMMENDED READING

- Ashkenas, R. and Manville, B. (2018). Leader's handbook: Make an impact, inspire your organization, and get to the next level. Harvard Business Review Press.
- Bazerman, M. H. (2020). A new model for ethical leadership. Harvard Business Review, September-October 2020, pp. 91-97.
- Grint, K. (2010). Leadership: A very short introduction. Oxford University Press.
- Ibarra, H. (2015). Act like a leader, think like a leader. Harvard Business Review Press.
- Kotter, J. (2001). What leaders really do. Harvard Business Review, December 2001, pp. 85-97.
- Lingo, E.L. & Maginen, K.L. (2020). A new prescription for power. Harvard Business Review, July- August 2020, pp. 67-75.

- Silva, A. (2016). What is leadership? Journal of Business Studies Quarterly, 2016, Volume 8, Number 1, pp. 1-5.
- Watkins, M.D. (2012). How managers become leaders. Harvard Business Review, June 2012, pp. 65-72.

# 11 MANAGERIAL COMMUNICATION

## 11.1 EFFECTIVE COMMUNICATION AND ITS IMPORTANCE

Communication is the process of dealing with someone in words or in writing. Managers depend on effective communication to achieve their business objectives. Communication will be effective when it conveys what the manager intends to convey. It is always necessary to remember the words of Peter Drucker: "Communication takes place in the mind of the listener, not in the mind of the speaker." Communication is effective if it has produced the desired changes or positive reactions in the recipient.

Effective communication is essential for the manager to be able to properly convey the vision they have of the organization and get the desired response from employees and customers. Effective communication must be timely and must have an appropriate level of detail.

Managers must ensure that all employees are well informed about the company's objectives and any aspects they need to know to conduct their work in pursuit of those objectives, but they must also encourage employees to send them their opinions and inform them properly about what is happening in operations and in the relationship with customers.

## 11.2 EFFECTIVE COMMUNICATION SKILLS

Managers' effective communication skills include:
- Know how to listen.
- Have empathy (placing oneself in the place of the other).
- Respect.
- Express themselves well orally and in writing.
- Have persuasion capacity.
- Demonstrate credibility and authority.

Unfortunately, many senior managers are not good communicators, they reserve information that is necessary for employees, they show incongruity between what they say and what they do and, what is worse, they are not interested in listening directly to employees, limited to reading reports or talking to middle managers.

Improving communication skills involves developing the assertiveness or self-esteem of the manager. Self-esteem is the degree of acceptance, respect, and appreciation that a person has of himself. An assertive person can communicate with people of all levels openly, directly, frankly, and appropriately.

## 11.2.1 Written communication

Written communication provides a record for reference and follow-up and facilitates the transmission of the same message to many people; however, a manager should put great care before writing something, as some people may misinterpret the meaning of the message and/or get upset with its content.

Before writing, managers need to think well about what they will say, organize their ideas, and avoid possible negative reactions. Written communication, in addition to being free of offenses or threats and of course spelling or grammatical errors, must be brief, clear, direct, precise, orderly, simple, and appropriate, so the readers can fix their attention on the most important.

## 11.2.2 Oral communication

Oral communication can be individual, in small group meetings, or in presentations to large audiences. When speaking in public, it is necessary for the manager to know his audience, understand his own capabilities, and be brief and simple.

Although some individual communications or meetings may be informal, it is desirable as a manager to:

- Prepare yourself; that is, define the objective (what you want to say, expose, or discuss) and properly structure the communication.
- Call the attention of interlocutors.
- Clearly explain the purpose of the communication
- State what you mean.
- Listen carefully to reactions (in case of individual communications or meetings).
- Close properly the session.

In one-on-one conversations and small group meetings managers should:

- Listen. Let others talk. Encourage them to express their opinions. Try to understand the perspectives of others, listening to them with an open mind and without prejudice
- Do not jump to conclusions. Allow others to clarify their opinions instead of rushing judgments
- Think about other people's reactions before expressing your ideas, trying to explain them as best as possible
- Explain the reasoning process followed to express your ideas
- Provide positive feedback. All people need motivation

Managers have many opportunities to communicate with other people, but they do not usually take advantage of them well. To take advantage of them, they must listen without distractions or prejudices, remain vigilant to pick up early signs of potential dangers, crises, and of opportunities.

As far as presenting to an audience is concerned, a rule of thumb is to define few ideas to convey, preferably no more than three, start by explaining what you want to say, then say it, and finally remember what you said.

It is important to speak naturally, without attempting unnecessary rhetorical resources, conveying confidence, and inspiring credibility.

The visual aids used in a presentation should provide interest, variety, and impact on the audience and facilitate the understanding and retention of the exposed.

## 11.3 COMMUNICATION IN THE COMPANY

In addition to improving their interpersonal communication skills, managers must learn to effectively manage communication within organizations. Effective communication is closely related to employee satisfaction. The lower the uncertainty, the greater the satisfaction. Effective communication helps to avoid distortions, ambiguities and inconsistencies that increase uncertainty and, therefore, have a negative effect on satisfaction. If there is no distorted communication, employees will understand management's messages about the goals and policies and strategies of the company or organization.

Managers should facilitate the best possible communication (top-down, bottom-up, and horizontal) between all levels of the organization:

- **Top-down communication** must have credibility, selectivity, and timeliness as characteristics.
- **Bottom-up communication** should not be restricted. The information that reaches the upper levels should be not only what senior managers want to hear.
- **Horizontal communication**, both formal and informal, like top-down and bottom-up communication, must be free of barriers that limit it.

Internal communication requires an informal structure of social networks, as well as a formal communication structure. The success and superior performance of the company will depend on its ability to properly combine the operation of both types of structures.

Corporate communication, internal and external, has

replaced the old function of "public relations" in companies and refers to how the organization communicates. It includes aspects of:

- Image.
- Identity.
- Corporate advertising.
- Media relations.
- Financial communication.
- Employee relations.
- Community relations.
- Relations with the government.
- Crisis communication.

To be effective, corporate communication should be clear, sincere, and opportune.

## 11.4 MEETINGS

Meetings, whether virtual or face-to-face, are necessary in the company to inform, exchange opinions and make decisions, but they must be effective. For meetings to be effective, you must:

- **Do not convene meetings that are not strictly necessary.** If a direct personal conversation, a phone call, or an email could allow to get the meeting's objectives, there should not be a

meeting. Sometimes regular meetings are necessary, such as at board meetings or shareholders' meetings, but there should be no periodic meetings.
- **Prepare the meetings**. Clearly establish their purpose, their agenda, and their duration. Only those whose presence is indispensable or convenient should participate in it. Meetings should not be long; in general, they should not last more than an hour
- **Properly direct the meetings**. Allow everyone to express their opinion but avoiding too many interventions from the same person, exceptionally long interventions or deviations from the topic or point under discussion, maintaining a good atmosphere, stimulating contrary opinions but avoiding conflicts between participants and inappropriate behaviors and controlling the time, so that the meeting does not last longer than expected
- **Make a good closing of the meeting**. Recall the decisions taken and the commitments agreed
- **Conduct an appropriate follow-up of the results of the meeting**. Verify that agreements are fulfilled.

## 11.5 RECOMMENDED READING

- Bryant, A, & Shares, K. (2021). Are you really listening? Harvard Business Review, March- April 2021, pp. 80-87.
- Munter, M. and Hamilton, L. (2013). Guide to managerial communication. Pearson, 10Th Edition.

# 12 MANAGERS

## 12.1 MANAGERS

Managers, executives, administrators, or directors are those responsible for directing the operations of a company, but in this chapter we call them managers.

### 12.1.1 The role of managers

Managers must make effective and efficient use of available resources (people, money, facilities, equipment) to obtain the results desired by the company.

### 12.1.2 Types of managers

In companies we can distinguish:

- **General managers**, who oversee the direction of an entire company or a business unit within it. In most cases, general managers are people who have excelled in the management of a specific function of the company or have rotated through various functions to acquire a global vision of the company.
- **Managers of specific functions or areas** (marketing, operations, finance, IT, human resources).

They are usually professionals specialized in disciplines related to the function they must direct.
- **Frontline managers or supervisors**, who – unlike the previous ones – do not have any managers among the employees under their supervision.

### 12.1.3 The work of managers

Not all managers do their jobs the same way. Some work preferentially in their offices, while others meet with people in their workplaces and even travel frequently to meet with employees and customers in other cities or countries. Some prefer written communication and others prefer to talk to others, by phone or in person. However, all must perform the functions defined by Henri Fayol in 1916:

- Plan.
- Organize.
- Direct.
- Coordinate.
- Control.

There are three dimensions of management, according to Henry Mintzberg:

- Routine management (meeting with others, reading reports, allocating resources, setting goals, assigning tasks, authorizing actions).
- Troubleshooting (troubleshooting setbacks arising from unplanned, unexpected, and often unwanted events).
- Leadership (lead, communicate, motivate, inspire, make changes).

### 12.1.4 The skills of managers

Management involves special competencies that not all people possess, and it is necessary to develop them to successfully exercise the direction of an organization. For example, while it is desirable for the general manager or director to possess sufficient knowledge of the business or activity to lead, they do not need to be the individual with the greatest technical competence within the organization. Thus, not necessarily the most competent doctor is the most qualified to run a hospital or the most qualified professor is the right person to run a university. Other types of qualities or competencies may be more relevant, such as:

- **Understanding of the environment**: ability to understand the environment in which it operates

(national environment, international environment).
- **Strategic thinking**: ability to know how to discern what is best suited for the organization.
- **Management skills**: ability to lead others (effective communication, team building and management, motivation, conflict management, development of other people).
- **Personal competencies**: ability to perform well in the different circumstances of life and work (integrity, effectiveness, management of uncertainty, creativity, leadership).

## 12.2 THE TRAINING OF MANAGERS

### 12.2.1 The knowledge needed for managers

In addition to a minimum of relevant technical knowledge, vision, intelligence, organizational capacity and skills for human relations, all managers of complex companies need to possess basic knowledge of economics, accounting, finance, and marketing, among other areas related to management.

As for the legal aspects related to the operation of companies, although it is necessary to have the advice of specialized lawyers, particularly in large companies, it is convenient that the manager acquires at least basic knowledge about commercial and labor laws, commercial transactions, contracts and property rights, crimes and damages, legal processes, and settlement of business disputes outside the courts.

## 12.2.2 Academic management training programs

Much of the knowledge that managers need they could get in practice, working in companies, but today it is essential to acquire them also through formal studies. A bachelor's degree in business administration may be sufficient to hold lower management positions in organizations, but to be able to aspire to higher positions today requires at least a Master of Business Administration (MBA). In general, the better the quality of the institution in which they study the MBA, the greater the chances for individuals to achieve success in their career.

In the first business schools, created during the nineteenth century, there were classes of economics, accounting, and commercial law, which were the fundamentals subjects to train an entrepreneur in that time. The curricula were subsequently enriched by advances in management theories and courses in finance, human resources, marketing, and operations, which today are part of any MBA program, gradually appeared during the twentieth century, especially in the second half of that century. In recent decades, courses in information systems and international business have been added.

After the MBA, you can pursue doctoral studies in business administration (DBA), which allow you to expand your knowledge and develop the ability to conduct research to improve the functioning of companies.

### 12.2.3 Practical training of the manager

The ideal training of a manager means that, after completing their basic formal studies, gradually assumes more demanding management positions within a company, and gets a promotion once demonstrates ability to achieve the expected results at the current level and potential to continue advancing towards higher levels.

The curiosity to learn and the willingness to continue studying, either formally or self-taught, will determine - to a considerable extent - that the person can ascend to the highest possible levels. Of course, companies do not always succeed in choosing the most capable to ascend within them and many subjective factors can intervene in this process, but bad decisions in this matter do not usually take long to demonstrate poor results and demand the necessary correctives.

## 12.3 THE EFFECTIVENESS OF MANAGERS

Not all managers perform their jobs efficiently. Some studies show that between 25 and 50% of people promoted to new roles do not perform well. In many cases, people come to these new roles without proper preparation and never manage to develop a true capacity to perform their functions. However, every day the competition for managerial positions is greater and there is a wide range of professionals with proven managerial experience or with an academic background that qualifies them to perform successfully, which allows companies to choose the right people to occupy the managerial positions within them. Companies can also develop their own managers, providing their potential employees with training and experience opportunities that enable them to progressively occupy positions of greater responsibility.

Directing is an overly complex task and doing it well implies a significant effort on the part of those who conduct this activity. Successful management involves a permanent development of the individual's abilities to:

- Correctly define the objectives and goals of the organization.
- Choose the appropriate strategy.
- Select the right collaborators and motivate them to give the best of their possibilities.
- Facilitating communication, teamwork and learning in the organization.

Peter Drucker asserted that effectiveness is not a gift, for no one is born effective. All managers must learn to be efficient. Drucker recommended these eight practices to be effective:

- **Ask yourself what you should do.** Instead of wondering what you want to do, as a manager you should start by asking yourself what you should do and, particularly, what must do now. When answering that question, if several tasks arise, you should focus on the task for which you are most prepared and delegate the other tasks.
- **Ask yourself what is in the company's best interest.** It is not a question of asking what is best for the shareholders, employees, or managers of the company separately, but what is best for the company.
- **Develop action plans.** Once you have answered the above questions you should map out your

plan. It must define what the desired results are, and in what timeframes, committing to those intentions and creating a system to control the results, understanding that the plan must be flexible and subjected to review according to the changes that occur. The action plan should serve as the basis for managing the manager's time.
- **Take responsibility for your decisions**. Managers must learn to make good decisions and know how to delegate their execution. Each decision must have a person responsible for making it and a deadline, as well as the identification of the people affected by the decision. Managers should ensure that they define these principles well and systematically review the execution of the decisions they have made.
- **Take responsibility for communicating**. Managers must ensure to communicate well their action plans. Communication helps the organization to perform better.
- **Focus on opportunities rather than problems**. Of course, solving problems does not produce results; what produces results is taking advantage of opportunities. Changes particularly are not threats but opportunities. The best people in the

organization must deal with the best opportunities.
- **Conduct productive meetings**. Most managers spend at least half their time in meetings, so they need to make sure they are productive. To conduct an effective meeting, it is necessary to define what type of meeting it is (to prepare a statement, to announce or approve something, to receive a report), to prepare the meeting according to its type, to limit the meeting to that purpose and to ensure that it does not last longer than necessary. Then, keeping a good follow-up to the meeting is just as important as the meeting itself.
- **Think and say "we" instead of "me"**. Although the manager is responsible, you must understand that you cannot think about your own needs and opportunities but must think about the needs and opportunities of the entire organization and have the trust of everyone and their participation and commitment.

Apart from following these recommendations, it is convenient for managers to learn how to efficiently use internal networks: by connecting soon to wider networks; energizing new connections; identifying those who can add value and help you close skills gaps; using networks to expand their influence; and prioritizing relationships that develop their experience at work.

## 12.4 RECOMMENDED READING

- Cross, B., Prior, G. & Sylvester, D. (2021). How to succeed quickly in a new role. Harvard Business Review, November- December 2021, pp. 60-69.
- Drucker, P. F. (2004). What makes an executive effective? Harvard Business Review, June 2004, pp. 58-63.
- Harvard Business Review (2017). Manager's handbook: The 17 skills leaders need to stand out. Harvard Business Review Press.
- Hendry, J. (2013). Management: A very short introduction. Oxford University Press.

# 13 MARKETING

## 13.1 THE MARKETING FUNCTION

Marketing is the function in the company of satisfying the needs of consumers or clients, creating value for them.

The main function of marketing is to link the company with its external environment; that is, to become a window of management to the outside. Marketing should act in a company as an engine for growth, leading the way to a more direct relationship with customers, new product opportunities and new markets.

Marketing integrates all the functions of the company and communicates directly with the consumer through advertising, salespeople, and other marketing activities.

## 13.2 MARKET RESEARCH

One of the main instruments of marketing management is market research. Market research is the systematic collection, recording and analysis of data regarding marketing problems, making use of methods such as focus groups, surveys, in-depth interviews, research in homes, and research in stores.

Market research involves an analysis of consumers, distributors, suppliers, the competition, and the company itself, looking for business opportunities in each market. The quality and depth of the market studies will define the possibility of success of the strategy designed from them.

Many of the best ideas come from observing major changes in the market environment. However, artificial intelligence has immense potential to design marketing strategies and many companies are already taking advantage of it. Artificial intelligence systems range from simple task automation to advanced machine learning models that allow you to recognize images, decipher texts, segment customers, and anticipate how consumers may respond to various initiatives, such as promotions.

## 13.3 MARKETING STRATEGY

Market research allows the company to define its marketing strategy. The marketing strategy involves the development of three main activities:

- Select the target market. The target market should be the one that considers the competition and fits best to the nature of the products and to the competitiveness of the company.

- Determine the desired positioning of the product in the minds of consumers in that market. Positioning, a concept proposed by Al Ries and Jack Trout in 1972, is the effort to identify a unique selling proposition for the product; that is, to establish in the mind of the consumer a clear, distinctive, and attractive position of the product in relation to competing products.
- Specify the marketing plan to conduct the necessary activities to achieve the desired positioning.

### 13.3.1 Market selection

The company must be sufficiently market-focused and consumer-oriented. In general, companies should not try to do everything in all markets, nor concentrate on large segments, but specialize and search for or target specific niches.

The company must decide in which markets it remains, in which reduce its participation, and in which new markets it ventures. In those markets in which it decides to act, it must proceed to the segmentation of the market; that is, to divide the market into segments and determine the segment or segments of interest to the company. To identify market segments, companies could use geographical, demographic, psychographic (lifestyles and personality), and behavioral (buying behaviors) criteria.

In the case of entry into new emerging markets, in which the forces of competition are in constant flux, companies could forget about differentiation and observe what others are doing in the market, taking from them what seems appropriate and experimenting incessantly until defining a flexible model to create value and waiting for the market to settle down to optimize it.

### 13.3.2 Marketing mix

The definition of marketing strategy includes making decisions about four elements, product, price, place, and promotion (called the 4P's), which together constitute the marketing mix, proposed in 1960 by Edmund Jerome McCarthy, then a professor at Harvard University and the Massachusetts Institute of Technology.

**The product**

The product is what the company offers to meet the needs of consumers. Products may be tangible (physical goods) or intangible (services). It is important to keep in mind that the product is not only the thing itself but the total package of benefits that the consumer receives when acquiring and using the product.

The higher the level of satisfaction generated by the product, the greater the success of the product. A common mistake in marketing is to be product-oriented, rather than consumer-oriented; in general, people are not interested in a product that their manufacturer considers to be of high quality but in a product that meets their needs.

The brand is the name or symbol used to specify the differentiation of the product and the value of the brand is the profit that can bring to the company. Brand personality is a set of human characteristics associated with a brand (sincerity, excitement, competence, sophistication, ruggedness). If a brand is not number one or number two, it may get out of the market.

An important aspect to consider in relation to a product is the stage of its life cycle in which it is located: introduction; growth; maturity; decline. The company's marketing strategies should include definitions of: which products should be retained and which should be abandoned; which product lines should be expanded and which should be reduced; what should be the priorities in the direction of new product development; how to differentiate the products; how the life cycle of each product affects plans; what are the most appropriate marketing strategies for each product; which products or services should be aggressively promoted; how to ensure that products exceed consumer expectations; etc.

### The price

The price is the monetary value expected for the product. When setting a price, not only its cost and usefulness matter, but also all the benefits derived from and/or included in it. The value of the product does not come from the effort that the company puts into its elaboration but from the benefits that the client thinks he will obtain from it, from what he can or wants to pay for the product and from what costs a similar product offered by other companies.

The elasticity of demand, i.e., changes in demand when prices vary, is a key factor to consider when assigning price to a product.

Some companies must legally protect themselves from distributors who offer unauthorized discounts, contrary to the companies' pricing policy.

### The place

The place is the market selected to offer the product. Market selection depends on examining the attractiveness of current or potential markets against the internal competencies and strengths of the company's products and services and those of its main competitors.

Marketing channels are the mechanisms that the company uses to reach its consumers or customers and include a variety of tasks ranging from demand generation to physical delivery of products. The distribution of the products can be direct (conducted by the company itself), indirect (conducted by a third party) or mixed; in any case, the company must analyze how its product can reach the consumer, how each player or participant in the distribution channel wins and who has the power in each channel.

### The promotion

The promotion is the set of activities through which the company communicates with the consumer so that he knows and buys the product. Although all elements of the marketing mix are important, promotion is the most important.

The promotional mix is composed of the controllable elements that the company must use to communicate its message: advertising; sales promotion; unpaid advertising; and personal sales. Advertising is the most effective form of promotion, and its purpose is not so much to inform the public but to create for people the need to acquire certain products to improve their well-being and be happier.

## 13.4 SALES

Marketing work should lead to the materialization of sales. The sale involves closing a deal with a specific customer, after marketing made the market want a product or service.

The sales process, whatever the sales procedure, implies the existence of distribution channels to get the product to the consumer, and there are multiple ways or channels of access to the consumer.

## 13.5 RELATIONS WITH THE CONSUMER

Relationship marketing is the process of building long- term connections and consumer trust. Today's marketing requires adequate consumer relationship management, to know their needs, understand their decision process to buy, ensure their satisfaction and retain them as a customer. The complexity of consumer behavior has led many companies and specialized firms to develop models of consumer behavior, which are simplifications that help organize thinking about consumers.

Marketing must shift from pushing individual products to building long-term relationships with consumers and the company must shift from measuring the profitability of products to measuring consumers' profitability.

Apart from technologies such as CRM (Customer Relationship Management), companies are making increasing use of social networks as marketing tools, facilitating not only bilateral communication between company and consumer but also communication between consumers.

Consumer management systems should stimulate their loyalty, as loyal consumers generate more profit than dissatisfied or simply satisfied consumers.

## 13.6 THE VALUE CREATION OF MARKETING

Marketing is supposed to create value for both the customer and the company, but measuring the value created is not easy. However, there are methods to measure the value created for customers in three areas (engagement, experience and sharing) and the value created for the company in three other areas (knowledge, strategy, and operational effectiveness).

## 13.7 NEW TECHNOLOGIES IN MARKETING

Marketing has a long tradition of adopting innovative technologies. Companies that invest more in innovative technologies are more agile and enjoy a strong competitive advantage over those that invest little or nothing.

Innovative technologies (artificial intelligence, virtual

reality/augmented reality, digital platforms, avatars, anthropomorphized "chatbots", visual computing methods, digital data capture technologies, data analytics) impact marketing in four major areas:

- Support new forms of interaction between consumers and businesses.
- Provide new types of data that enable new analytical methods.
- Create marketing innovations.
- Require new strategic marketing frameworks.

## 13.8 RECOMMENDED READING

- Comstock, B., Gulati, R., and Liguori, S. (2010). Unleashing the power of marketing. Harvard Business Review, October 2010, pp. 90-98.
- Davenport, T., Guha, A. and Grewal, D. (2021). How to design an AI marketing strategy. Harvard Business Review, July- August 2021, pp. 42-47.
- Hoffman, D. L., Moreau, C. P., Stremersch, S. & Wedel, M. (2022). The rise of innovative technologies in marketing: A framework and outlook. Journal of Marketing, 2022, Vol. 86 (1), pp. 1-6.
- Kotler, P. and Armstrong, G. (2020). Principles of marketing. Pearson.

- Kotler, P., Kartajaya, H. and Setiawan, I. (2021). Marketing 5.0: Technology for humanity. Wiley.
- Le Meunier- Fitzhugh, K. (2021). Marketing: A very short introduction. Oxford University Press.
- Levitt, T. (1960/2004). Marketing myopia. Harvard Business Review, reprinted July 2004.
- McCarthy, E. J. (1960). Basic marketing: A managerial approach. Richard D. Irwin, Inc.
- McDonald, R. & Eisenhardt, K. (2020). The new-market conundrum. Harvard Business Review, May- June 2020, pp. 74-83.
- Oswald, A. (2020). Advertising makes us unhappy. Harvard Business Review, January- February 2020, pp. 32-33.
- Overgoor, G., Chica, M., Rand, W. & Weishampel, A. (2019). Letting the computers take over: Using AI to solve marketing problems. California Management Review, 2019, Vol. 61(4) pp. 156-185.
- Rodríguez- Vilá, O., Bharadwaj, S., Morgan, N. A. and Mitra, S. (2020). Is your marketing organization ready for what's next? Harvard Business Review, November- December 2020, pp. 105-113.

- Rust, R. T., Moorman, C., and Bhalla, G. (2010). Rethinking marketing. Harvard Business Review, January- February 2010, pp. 94- 101.
- Silk, A.J. (2006). What is marketing? Harvard Business School Press.

# 14 OPERATIONS

## 14.1 THE ROLE OF OPERATIONS MANAGEMENT

Operations management is the function responsible for performing the activities necessary to produce and offer the company's products or services. The term production management refers particularly to the management of manufacturing processes.

Operations management must work in conjunction with marketing, finance, and other departments to achieve the best possible performance of the company.

Some of the critical decisions of operations management are as follows:

- What goods and services should we offer our customers?
- What processes, equipment and technology do we need to deliver those goods and services?
- What should we do ourselves and what can we order from a supplier?
- Where should we locate our facilities?
- How should we schedule our operations?
- How much inventory should we have of each product?
- How should we perform maintenance?

- How can we create a work environment that facilitates productivity?
- How will we ensure the quality of our goods and services?
- How will we continuously improve our processes?

## 14.2 PRODUCT DESIGN AND PRODUCTION PROCESS

Although the operations to develop and offer products and services have certain similarities, the operations of production or manufacture of products are usually much more complex and require a more detailed analysis.

To conduct production operations, it is necessary to start with the design of the product and the selection of the production process. Once you design the product and select the production process, you should define the supply chain and the location of the factories or production facilities.

## 14.3 OPERATIONS PLANNING

Operations planning should be based on an estimate or forecast of future demand for products. No matter the method used to forecast demand, qualitative or quantitative, the results give production management only a starting point. Along the way it will be necessary to make the necessary adjustments to adapt to the realities of sales.

## 14.4 PRODUCTION PLANNING

The company must plan its production in the long, medium, and short term:

**Long-term production planning**, usually for the next 2 to 5 years, should start from a forecast or estimate of demand for that planning horizon, based on qualitative models (Delphi method, historical data, nominal group technique, market research) and/or quantitative models (time series analysis, regression analysis, economic models).

**Medium-term production planning**, usually for next year, involves forecasting demand for the company's products during that period and defining how to meet that demand. Medium-term demand forecasting can be based on the application of the same long-term demand forecasting methods, but it can also use information from contracts made by the company to deliver products to certain customers, if such contracts exist.

**Short-term production planning**, usually for the next week or month, consists of foreseeing in sufficient detail the activities to achieve the desired production goals in that period.

## 14.5 LOGISTICS AND THE SUPPLY CHAIN

Logistics is the function of the company to take the right product, to the right place, in the right conditions of quantity and quality, at the right time, and with minimal costs. Logistics management deals with the movement and storage of materials, components and intermediate and finished products throughout the production process.

The logistics chain or supply chain is the set of activities, facilities and means necessary to conduct the production process from the search for raw materials to the delivery of the product to the final consumer.

Supply chain management consists of the integration of activities, cooperation, coordination, and exchange of information throughout the entire chain, from suppliers to end customers.

Companies could modernize the supply chain improving its efficiency, by collecting readily available data and using advanced analytical techniques to understand and predict the behavior of customers and suppliers and optimize decision-making about inventory, production, and procurement (purchasing), including some automation to improve existing processes or introduce new processes.

Another way to improve supply chain efficiency is by

applying the circular business model, which involves recovering used products and reusing or recycling them. To create this model, maintain ownership of the product, extend its useful life, and design it for recycling.

When it comes to the supply of raw materials, it is particularly important that the company establishes long-term agreements with its suppliers, both high and low level, and is concerned with ensuring that all of them meet the required social and environmental standards of sustainability.

Globalization is increasingly stimulating specialization, so global companies prefer to do certain things in certain locations, rather than do it all in one place.

Internationalization implies greater complexity in supply chains that if not effectively managed can result in higher costs. The main challenges faced by internationalized companies with this increasing complexity of their supply chains are:

- Longer lead times, with consequent loss of flexibility and responsiveness.
- Higher inventory levels (security, cycle and in transit), leading to higher inventory maintenance costs.

- Increased risk associated with international operations (problems during transport, geopolitical risk).

## 14.6 THE LOCATION OF PRODUCTION PLANTS

An especially important aspect in defining the supply chain is the location of the manufacturing plant or plants. This is an extremely major decision for the success of a manufacturing company and depends on many factors (economic, environmental, legal, safety), which can have different relative importance for each industry and for each company.

The location of manufacturing plants could have two phases:

**Macro localization.** In this phase, the company analyzes a wide geographical area to set its production or service operations. The main factors to consider in the macro localization are cultural aspects, legal and governmental restrictions, incentives for the location of enterprises, environmental aspects, location in industrial parks, energy generation centers, consumer market and input supply sources, and availability and cost of land.

**Micro localization.** When the company has chosen the macro location that is convenient for its operations, then it will proceed to conduct a detailed study of the possible cities, towns or sites of its interest that are within the area. The main factors to consider in the micro location are cost of the land, availability of public services, availability of labor, and acceptable urban and/or rural access and transport routes

In the case of multinational or global companies, they must decide the location of their production plants considering not only the aforementioned factors, but also those related to the conditions of transport of inputs and finished products between countries, the customs and commercial barriers that may exist, and the risks of political conflicts between countries that may affect the functioning of the logistics chain.

## 14.7 PRODUCTION METHODS

In general, production methods are of three basic types:

- **Continuous process.** It is a repetitive method, for high production volumes, used when it comes to a highly standardized product.
- **Assembly line.** It is a progressive manufacturing process, a little more flexible and less continuous, in which workers add parts (usually interchangeable) as the product in manufacture moves from station to station, until achieving final assembly.

- **Manufacturing on demand or according to demand (job shop).** It is a process in which the company manufactures specific products for one customer at a time. Each work order is different, but the same basic equipment and instruments are employed in each order.

## 14.8 OPERATIONS RESEARCH

Operations research or management science is a set of mathematical and statistical techniques discovered or improved by the Allies during World War II (Great Britain, United States, Soviet Union) to maximize military production. After the war, companies used those techniques to improve decision-making and optimize their processes. Two of the most frequently used techniques to solve operational problems of companies are linear programming and queue theory.

### 14.8.1 Linear programming

In many operations of the company, the problem arises of optimally allocating the available resources. The linear programming method could help to solve some of the problems of this type.

Linear programming aims to determine how to

allocate available resources in a way that maximizes or minimizes an objective function (e.g., utility or cost) subject to certain constraints on the use of resources. Both the objective function and the constraints are linear equations.

This method is linear because it assumes that the relationship between the variables is such that when one increases or decreases the other increases or decreases in the same proportion (straight line).

Specialists use matrix algebra and computers to solve linear programming problems; however, simple problems, restricted to only two variables, have graphic solutions.

The transport method is a particular application of linear programming, which aims to minimize the cost of transport from several origins to different destinations.

### 14.8.2 Queue theory

Queues or waiting phenomena are common situations in the operations of companies; for example, trucks waiting space for loading or unloading, and customers waiting for service. To eliminate queues, companies would have to invest in excessive capacity costs of loading or unloading facilities, service installations, etc. Therefore, the best thing they can do is design their facilities so that the queues are moderate, avoiding excessive waiting costs or inconvenience from suppliers or customers.

In general, companies best analyze queue problems using simulation models. However, it is possible to use simpler methods, based on queuing theory, at least as a preliminary form of analysis, estimating the average waiting times corresponding to different capacities of the service facilities and then selecting a capacity that allows reasonable average waiting times.

Queue theory is the mathematical study of queues or waiting lines within a system. A queuing system has two main components: the queue and the service installation. To study a queuing system, it is necessary to know or estimate the distribution of customer arrival, the customer service policy (for example, "first to arrive, first to be served"), the average service time and its variability, the number of servers or service stations, the cost for the customer to wait and the cost of service. In general, the optimal capacity of the analyzed system is one that allows to minimize the total cost of operation (waiting cost + service cost).

Queuing theory shows that when utilization approaches system capacity, waiting times increase exponentially, making it necessary to increase the number of service stations and/or decrease the average service time.

## 14.9 INVENTORIES

In the execution of operations, it is necessary to make decisions regarding inventories. Inventories are the raw materials and finished products stored in the company. Inventory should be as low as possible, and some very efficient companies try to get materials to arrive just in time for production, as Toyota began using in 1952.

In general, companies do not want to have inventory of raw materials or finished products, to avoid both the cost of storage and the cost of owning those materials or products without providing them with benefits. However, companies need these inventories in many situations, for example:

- Because the supply of raw materials or products can fail, affecting production or sales.
- Because the nature of the business demands it (for example: department stores, supermarkets, bookstores).

The optimal size of inventory depends on the characteristics and strategy of the company, as well as the times and costs of replenishment and inventory rotation. In factories or production plants, they use MRP (Material Requirements Planning) systems for work planning and inventory control.

## 14.10 PRODUCTIVITY

Productivity is the measure of efficiency of the production process and is determined as the relationship between the products obtained and the inputs or resources used. In general, production processes go through a learning process and as the company acquires greater experience in its field it increases its efficiency or productivity and reduces its unit costs.

## 14.11 QUALITY

Quality is to meet the requirements specified by the customer. This means that to successfully conduct the production process and guarantee quality it is necessary to know very well the characteristics of the product or service that the client expects to receive.

In companies, quality assurance is usually based on checking that work processes align with the needs of customers, generate the desired results, and are well documented, certified by an independent audit firm, and properly applied to each production process.

Japanese companies created the Total Quality Model (TQM) in the 1950s, with the help of W. Edwards Deming. The basic principles of the total quality model are as follows:

- Committed leadership.
- Customer focus.
- Ongoing education and training.
- Participation and empowerment.
- Teamwork.
- Recognition.
- Effective communication.

The total quality model makes use of various methodological tools, such as:

- Continuous improvement.
- Quality handbooks.
- Measurements and statistical control.
- Other tools (check sheet, cause-effect diagram, flowchart, control graph, histogram, correlation graph, Pareto graph).

## 14.12 CONTINUOUS IMPROVEMENT AND REENGINEERING

Companies cannot be satisfied with achieving a satisfactory level of efficiency in their production processes and the quality of their products or services and staying at that level. Changes in the environment and the constant harassment of the competition force companies to continuously improve these processes and the quality of their products or services.

Reengineering involves a thorough review of operations, a redesign, a rethinking of the company to promote and adopt radical changes in which the customer and the competition are the fundamental triggers of the process.

The advantages and disadvantages of reengineering depend on how companies apply it. If reengineering is a review of the company's processes, it can be especially useful to improve them. But if you interpret reengineering as "clean slate", that is, as re-creating the company from scratch, as it was in the nineties, it can be a disaster, as indeed it was. In fact, reengineering can be extremely negative if it involves mass layoffs and radical transformation of the company, affecting the people who work in it. On the other hand, it can be positive if limited to a review of the company's processes, with the intention of improving them, seeking only minor or at least gradual changes that affect people less.

## 14.13 RECOMMENDED READING

- Atasu, A., Dumas, C. and Van Wassenhove, L. N. (2021). The circular business model. Harvard Business Review, July- August 2021, pp. 72-80.

- Bouchery, R.J., Tijms, H., and Braaksma, A. (2021). Operations research: Introduction to models and methods. WSPC.
- McDonough, A. (2020). Operations and supply chain management: Essentials you always wanted to know. Vibrant Publishers.
- Simchi- Levi, D. & Timmermans, K. (2021). To simpler way to modernize your supply-chain. Harvard Business Review, September- October 2021, pp. 133-141.
- Villena, V.H., and Gioia, D.A. (2020). A more sustainable supply chain. Harvard Business Review, March- April 2020, pp. 84-93.

# 15 ORGANIZATIONAL BEHAVIOR

## 15.1 THE CONCEPT OF ORGANIZATIONAL BEHAVIOR

Organizational behavior is the study of the conduct of people in organizations, to achieve forms of conduct that favor the best performance of those organizations. The study of organizational behavior teaches how to deal with human challenges in the workplace.

## 15.2 MICRO AND MACRO ORGANIZATIONAL BEHAVIOR

Although it is not a classification used by all authors, one can distinguish between "micro" and "macro" organizational behavior.

Initially, "micro" was the study of individual and group behavior and "macro" the study of the influence of the organization on the behavior of people. However, as it became aware that modern organizations function as open systems and, therefore, their behavior is greatly influenced by the environment, the term "micro" was applied to the study of organizational behavior related mainly to internal variables (individual differences, group dynamics, structure, organizational culture, power processes and politics, etc.) and the term "macro" was reserved for the influence of the environment (demography, globalization, technology, socio-cultural forces, political and legal forces, etc.) on organizational behavior.

### 15.2.1 Individual behavior

The actions of individuals determine organizational behavior. Organizations may try to condition that behavior through policies and rules that set out what to do and what not to do, but it is virtually impossible to regulate everything, especially in a large enterprise. Individuals' personality differences, values, aptitudes and attitudes, discretion, greater or lesser commitment to the organization, and other variables of individual behavior will always be present and influence organizational behavior.

### 15.2.2 The influence of groups and organization on individual behavior

People often modify their behavior when working in a group or when working in a certain organization:

Groups affect the individual behavior since each person usually will have to adjust their conduct to the characteristics of the other persons in the group

Organizations influence the employee's behavior through formal ways (policies and norms) or informal ways (organizational culture)

Therefore, organizational behavior is the result of a complex interaction between individuals, groups, and the organization.

### 15.2.3 The influence of the environment on organizational behavior

But it is not just internal factors that influence organizational behavior. Among the external factors that have an influence on organizational behavior, there are the following:

- **Demographic changes**: the ageing of the labor force, cultural diversity, and the increase in the proportion of women in the labor market.
- **Globalization**, which has made employees of almost any organization found themselves in the need to interact with different people in race, language, culture, religion, or ideology, who fear losing their jobs and jobs due to the intensification of competition and must, in addition, work more hours, which, together with the need to collaborate with different people, usually leads to a bad organizational climate.
- **Information and communication technologies**, which relieve work and facilitate communication,

but make people work longer hours, dehumanize the work environment, and create tensions in the workforce due to differences in adaptation to them between young and old people.
- **The socio-cultural forces**, including religion, ideology, and culture in general of the society in which the company operates.
- **The political-legal forces**. No organization can isolate itself from its environment and ignore what is happening in it, including politics and laws. Politics and laws affect all people and all organizations.

## 15.3 THE MOTIVATION

Motivation is the impulse that induce a person to behave in a certain way. This stimulus determines the effort a person is willing to make to achieve a given goal.

### 15.3.1 The importance of motivation for work

Motivation for work has significant importance in the behavior of people in an organization. Motivated people, unlike unmotivated ones, will have positive behaviors, characterized by a high dedication and commitment to the objectives of the organization.

Motivation usually begins when people perform jobs they like and/or they think are worthwhile. Many times, it is not easy to allow people to work on what they like or what they feel is worthwhile, but if failing to do so it will be difficult to have motivated people.

In addition, many companies have an environment and organizational climate unfavorable to employee motivation. Managers tend to distrust employees, their loyalty, commitment, and dedication, do not care about finding out their needs and their mood, treat them as disposable resources, and threaten and admonish or sanction them without justified reasons.

### 15.3.2 Needs and motivation

There are many theories about motivation. The best known relate motivation to the satisfaction of the individual's needs. Abraham Maslow, at the City University of New York, claimed in 1943 that the human being has higher needs for personal fulfillment and growth, and that these are only satisfied after having addressed the basic needs, whether existential or physiological.

David McClelland later proposed that people have three types of needs: achievement, power, and affiliation. Although it is possible that in many people the three types of needs coexist, usually one of them prevail.

### 15.3.3 The main motivating factors

Frederick Herzberg, a professor at the University of Utah, considered it necessary, in 1968, to distinguish between motivational factors and demotivating factors. Motivational factors are those that contribute to job satisfaction (for example, a promotion or a recognition) and demotivating factors, which he called "hygiene factors," are those whose absence contributes to dissatisfaction at work (for example, a safe place to work or a salary that allows you to live properly). To favor motivation, companies should maximize motivating factors and minimize demotivating ones.

Around the same time, Victor Vroom proposed his theory of expectations, according to which motivation depends on people's expectations; that is, the relationship between the effort they must make to achieve a result and the benefit they can achieve with that result.

Among the main motivating factors of employees there are the following:

- Interesting work that presents challenges for the person.

- Remuneration appropriate to the work performed.
- Opportunities for progress in the company.
- Projection and social prestige because of the work done.
- Recognition of superior and co-workers.

The absence or failures in the motivational factors are usually causes of employee demotivation, including poor relationships with the boss or supervisor, perception of unfair or inequitable treatment, excessive workload, and interference of work with the needs of their personal lives and family relationships.

In general, people need to feel useful and receive recognition for their work and managers need to create an environment in which all members can contribute to the best of their ability. When managers have confidence in people and expect them to be motivated, people often respond appropriately to those expectations.

### 15.3.4 The influence of participation and delegation on motivation

The success of the company depends on the participation of people and managers must delegate power ("empowerment") so that everyone contributes to the work. It is necessary to allow employees to make decisions that affect the customer and customer service without needing to seek prior approval. To make this possible, senior manager must not only be willing to compromise part of their day-to-day decision-making, but they must also ensure that employees at the appropriate levels have access to all the information they need to make informed decisions. The key to the future is communication.

## 15.4 TEAMS

In modern organizations, individuals cannot achieve any major goal. Hence the need to create working groups to achieve different objectives: solving problems, implementing projects, creating new products, or improving processes.

### 15.4.1 The difference between a working group and a team

It is a mistake to confuse a workgroup with a team. A working group is just a group of people who work together, in the same unit or department of the company; for a working group to become a team, it is necessary that its members complement each other and cooperate closely with each other to achieve a common goal.

## 15.4.2 The effectiveness factors of the teams

The effectiveness of teams depends on many factors, including the following:

- The selection of members, so that, despite the desirability of a small group size, there is an adequate diversity of talents, skills, values, and personalities in accordance with the purposes pursued.
- The appointment of a competent leader, of proven effectiveness, capable of earning the trust and respect of the members of the team and the rest of the organization, seeking the integration of the complementary skills of the team members to achieve the proposed objectives and effectively manage the conflicts that may arise during the performance of the team.
- The definition of a common purpose, with clear, feasible and shared objectives and the definition of collective and individual responsibilities to achieve those objectives.
- Support to the team by the organization, particularly by senior management, in terms of resource allocation, provision of information and collaboration of other units when required by the team

- The availability of time to achieve a common learning process and team consolidation.
- The generation of an environment of trust and commitment within the team, in which its members believe that they can achieve the expected results, share a common mental model of teamwork, are able to improvise, trust each other and feel safe.
- Frequent communication and exchange of information between team members.

### 15.4.3 Problems in team building

It is not easy to turn a workgroup into an effective team. There are several factors that hinder the formation of a team, including:

- Many times, the members of working groups are not complementary in their skills, or they do not have the willingness and ability to collaborate and cooperate with others.
- Many workgroup leaders are not really leaders; that is, they are not able to inspire trust among group members or properly direct them toward achieving common goals.

- But what most threatens the formation and success of a team is the business practice of evaluating the performance of each employee based on individual and not collective results. The conflicts of interest that result from the adoption of this practice simply make no one have an interest in collaborating or cooperating with another, because there is nothing to encourage them to do so and, on the contrary, they can neglect the achievement of their individual objectives if they set out to help others.

### 15.4.4 The challenges of virtual teams

Virtual teams present special challenges, due to the relative isolation of their members. The leaders of these teams must make significant efforts, usually supported by useful information and communication technology systems, to maintain the motivation, cohesion, and effectiveness of the team. A viable solution to overcome the challenges faced by virtual team leaders is to delegate authority and decision-making to team members, advising them rather than directing them and regularly seeking their support to solve problems.

## 15.5 POWER AND POLITICS

In business, as in government and in all other human organizations, there is a struggle for power; that is, there is political activity. Many people try to climb positions, not always to help the company solve its problems and achieve better goals, but simply to have more power. In that struggle for power, some want to play fair; that is, they try to convince others, respect all other participants, and act transparently and honestly. But there are others who lie, deceive, and try to get rid of their rivals by any means. Everyone chooses the methods they employ to take part in politics, but honest people who decide to acquire and use power, in companies or in any other field, should try to do so with the methods they consider worthy and appropriate, although many others do not.

On the other hand, managers must understand that they should not use power for their own benefit or simply to control their subordinates, but to mobilize their energy and commitment based on the objectives of the organization and society.

## 15.6 CORPORATE CULTURE

Corporate culture is the set of principles, beliefs and values that guide the action of the members of an organization.

## 15.6.1  The role of corporate culture

Corporate culture is how an organization does things, guided by the incentives that it applies. It is a system of social control that guides employees to understand the "reality" and to know how to relate and collaborate with others; that is, it serves as glue to integrate the members of an organization.

## 15.6.2  The influence of national culture on corporate culture

The culture of a company, although it has some elements that differentiate it from its environment, is not and cannot be alien to the culture of society or the country in which it conducts its operations. The people who come to work at the company or those who relate to it for one reason or another bring the cultural elements of the societies from which they come and act. This situation is much more complex in the case of global companies, which although they can create certain principles, beliefs, and values common among their members around the world, they can never manage to eliminate the cultural differences that exist between their subsidiaries in Europe, Africa, Asia, Oceania, North America, and Latin America.

### 15.6.3 The development of an appropriate culture

Performance measurement, compensation systems and work practices must align with the principles of fostering learning and innovation to achieve the promotion of an appropriate organizational culture. The company's top executives should stimulate criticism and initiative within the organization, free exchange of ideas and experimentation, and create an environment in which people feel safe and not threatened.

### 15.6.4 Culture conducive to change

Corporate culture, formed in tradition, has been an obstacle or anchor to change; however, it is possible to have a culture that helps us adapt and does not anchor us in the past. A healthy culture, which allows adaptation to change, is one in which your managers really care about their customers, shareholders and employees and truly valued and encouraged initiative and leadership at any level of the organization.

Some business cultures and some national cultures facilitate change processes more than others. One of the actions that reduce resistance to change is to promote continuous learning. Many times, people resist change for fear of not possessing the necessary knowledge to adapt to the new situation. A corporate culture that encourages learning, as well as innovation, is a culture conducive to change.

## 15.7 THE ORGANIZATIONAL CLIMATE

The organizational climate is the set of characteristics of the environment of the organization that determine the mood of its members. A good organizational climate is one in which the members of the organization feel at ease and work with enthusiasm. Like the weather, the organizational climate can vary and worsen; in this case, usually by decisions made by senior management against the interests and expectations of employees. The organizational climate may be uniform throughout the organization or may vary among different units or departments, usually in relation to the behavior of the corresponding manager or director.

## 15.8 RECOMMENDED READING

- Griffin, R. W. & Philips, J.M. (2020). Organizational behavior. Cengage, 13th edition.
- Herzberg, F. (1968). Again: how do you motivate your employees? Harvard Business Review, January- February 1968, pp. 13-22.

- Johns, G. (2006). The essential impact of context on organizational behavior. Academy of Management Review, 2006, Vol. 31, No. 2, pp. 386-408.
- Lingo, E.L. and McGinn, K.L. (2020). A new prescription for power. Harvard Business Review, July- August 2020, pp. 67-75.
- Pfeffer, J. & Veiga, J. F. (1999). Putting people first for organizational success. The Academy of Management Executive, May 1999 v13 i2 p37(1).
- Sharma, P. N., D'Innocenzo, L. and Kirkman, B. L. (2021) Why leaders resist empowering virtual teams. Sloan Management Review, Fall 2021, Vol. 63 (1).

# 16 ORGANIZATIONAL CHANGE

## 16.1 IMPORTANCE OF CHANGE AND INNOVATION

Companies live in an incredibly competitive environment, which also changes permanently. To survive and succeed in that environment, companies must change to adapt or anticipate to new realities.

But, in addition to simply changing, companies must innovate; that is, to create new things that have an impact on the market. One of the most effective business strategies is differentiation; that is, perceived as different in the market, so that potential customers prefer their products and services to perceive them as different and better than those of other companies. To achieve differentiation, companies must innovate, getting ahead of competitors.

## 16.2 ORGANIZATIONAL CHANGE

### 16.2.1 Organizational change

Organizational change means not any change that occurs in an organization but a change that affects the entire organization or company. Organizational change is the modification of one or more of the main components of an organization or company: strategy, structure, systems, people, organizational skills, managerial style, culture. In changes of some importance, it is highly likely that when modifying one of these components, the company must adjust the other components to maintain the necessary harmony between them.

Although all companies in the world seem to be in permanent processes of change, to respond to the great variations in the environment, the truth is that most change efforts fail or at least cost more, take longer, or do not achieve all the expected results. In addition, organizational change efforts are always accompanied by congruence issues, needs, conflicts, and feelings of loss. For these reasons, before starting any process of change the organization must be very sure of its need and viability. In addition, change must be thoughtfully planned.

Unfortunately, many changes that companies make are not necessary, are not timely or are not well planned. For example, usually:

- Changing the organizational structure when the problem may not be there, also underestimating the adjustment that this change implies in other components of the organization.

- Introducing information systems (technology), sometimes just to be fashionable, without checking if these changes are necessary.
- Superposing processes of change in organizations, generated by different individuals with power in them, creating an environment of confusion and wear and tear that usually harms efficiency, productivity, and organizational climate.
- Initiating change processes without an adequate plan to carry them out; that is, without defining in detail the activities to perform and the responsibilities of their execution, as well as without identifying the necessary resources and risks that may impede the success of the process.

Apart from initiating unnecessary, inopportune, or poorly planned change processes, there is also the possibility of delaying necessary changes due to lack of information. In general, when there is abundant information in a market about the need for a change, it is too late to start it, since it is most likely that competitors have gone ahead. For this reason, executives usually initiate the most opportune changes, can act with less information, and take more risks, without having to convince many stakeholders of the need for change.

## 16.2.2 Models of organizational change

To facilitate change processes, it is convenient to make use of one of the different change management models available.

Kurt Lewin, then a professor at the University of Iowa, proposed in 1939 the first model of change. His model defines change as the use of the forces that help change take place, acting against the forces that prevent change from occurring. Lewin considers three stages in the process of change: a) Defrost; b) Change; c) Refreezing.

Among the most recent models of change is the one proposed in 1996 by Professor John Kotter of Harvard University, who suggested following these eight steps when leading a change:

1. Establish a sense of urgency of the need for change.
2. Form a powerful driving coalition.
3. Create a vision.
4. Communicate that vision.
5. Empower others to act on that vision and remove obstacles to the process of change.
6. Plan and create short-term victories in the desired direction.

7. Consolidate improvements and generate more changes.
8. Institutionalize changes in organizational culture.

### 16.2.3 Resistance to change

In all processes of change, occurs resistance in at least part of the organization. To overcome this resistance you must, according to Kotter, follow these steps (the first three are essential and the other three are optional, depending on your need):

1. Educate and communicate (about change)
2. Participate and involve
3. Facilitate and support
4. Negotiate and agree
5. Manipulating and co-opting (giving an individual an attractive role in the process of change)
6. Coercion (explicitly or implicitly)

### 16.2.4 Organizational development

Organizational development is the set of activities that the company can perform, usually with the support of consultants or advisors, to improve its efficiency and facilitate change processes.

Organizational development involves the execution

of interventions in different areas of the company, to overcome the problems that may exist in them, improve their efficiency, and support the changes that are necessary. Interventions could be:

- Interventions in the human process (coaching, training, and development).
- Techno-structural interventions (structural design, restructuring, reengineering).
- Interventions in human resource management (performance management, development, and employee support).
- Strategic interventions (strategic change, mergers and acquisitions, alliances).

### 16.2.5 The ability of companies to change

In today's rapidly evolving environment, companies need to know their ability to change. However, it is not easy to determine this capacity because there are few systems to measure it. One of the proposed systems of measuring the capacity for change considers the determination of strengths and weaknesses in nine traits and abilities:

- Purpose.
- Address.
- Connectivity.

- Capacity.
- Dynamism.
- Diffusion.
- Development.
- Action.
- Flexibility.

## 16.3 INNOVATION

### 16.3.1 The concept of innovation

The most significant and impactful change a company can make is innovation. Many definitions of innovation exist, but in general:

"Innovation is the set of efforts aimed at the development of new products and services or the change in the technical, administrative and commercial processes of the company, in order to generate a positive impact on the market".

### 16.3.2 Types of innovation

Innovation can be:

**Technological or commercial**, depending on whether they are new products or services or new structures, systems, or processes.

**Incremental or radical**, building on existing knowledge and allowing existing products to remain competitive, or relying on new quite different knowledge and making existing products uncompetitive. Radical innovation is the same as a revolutionary, discontinuous, drastic, disruptive, or competence-destroying innovation.

### 16.3.3  The innovation process

The innovation process follows the following phases:
- Generation (conception of the idea of innovation).
- Elaboration (definition of innovation).
- Advocacy (seeking support and funding).
- Implementation (development of innovation).

In general, the innovation process is uncertain and is based on improvisation and the exploration of different paths or options, until achieving the desired results. As a result, these processes usually require a lot of effort, time and money, and many different skills and competences.

Innovation requires experimentation and mistakes. You cannot innovate without experimentation, and you cannot experiment without making mistakes. Very innovative companies are not afraid to make mistakes, even to launch products that can be failures. The important thing is that the mistake results from an honest effort to prove something, combined with a diligent attempt to execute it well.

The innovation process improves when innovators establish alliances with each other and with company managers, sharing a vision and creating a sense of collaboration that varies according to the phase of the process.

### 16.3.4 The development of a company's innovation capacity

The capacity for innovation of a company depends on its resources, processes, values, and its capacity for change. These factors include technological and market knowledge, the people who compose it, belonging to a dynamic and competitive sector of economic activity and the existence of a culture favorable to change.

A company can become innovative by following different paths or routes, but in many cases the following happens:

1. Changes in the characteristics of the environment stimulate the adoption of a change strategy if the company has sufficient resources and capabilities to innovate.

2. Once there is a greater willingness to change and innovation in the company, because of changes in the characteristics of the environment, market orientation is a fundamental determinant of the capacity for innovation, if there is an effective leadership that promotes the free exchange of ideas and creates an environment favorable to change.
3. By creating an environment conducive to change, and promoting the free exchange of ideas, research, and development projects, favored by information technology, result in important innovations for the company. These innovation projects in the company achieve greater success when they have an adequate definition and understanding of the mission and goals of the project, an effective consultation with the project user, and sufficient support from senior management.
4. Finally, the company's performance improves when it effectively conducts innovation activities and consolidates a dynamic capacity for innovation.

### 16.3.5 The organization for innovation

Most large companies have business units, each with its their own set of functions. In this way, the leaders of each unit lack a deep understanding of the rest of the organization and the company finds it difficult to conduct innovation processes that require collaboration between different units. One solution, as Apple did, is to organize the company according to functions, making it easier for leaders to be functionally collaborative and deeply aware of the details. Instead of general managers overseeing managers, Apple is a company of experts leading experts.

## 16.4 CULTURE CONDUCIVE TO CHANGE AND INNOVATION

To foster change and innovation in companies, their top executives must become leaders of these processes and foster a culture that stimulates creativity, initiative, questioning of what exists, cooperation, collaboration, teamwork, and experimentation.

This culture is the opposite of what prevails in most companies, so their leaders have the great challenge of modifying the existing culture if they want to drive change and innovation. Leaders should create an environment of curiosity and experimentation.

In general, cultural change is the most difficult of

organizational changes and requires the commitment and persistent action of the company's top executives. This process involves identifying and making use of the networks of influence in the organization; that is, knowing how employees interact in informal networks with those who share their values and with the people they consider their leaders or those they take seriously into account.

## 16.5 ORGANIZATIONAL LEARNING AND KNOWLEDGE MANAGEMENT

To change, innovate and succeed, organizations must be able to learn new knowledge, with two purposes: to improve and to transform.

### 16.5.1 Learning organizations

According to Peter Senge, director of the Center for Organizational Learning at the Massachusetts Institute of Technology, learning organizations are "organizations where people constantly develop their ability to create the results they really want to achieve; where new ways of thinking can grow; where there is collective aspiration; and where people learn continuously".

Companies can learn from themselves, the environment and partners or allies. The rapidly changing nature of today's business environment makes continuous employee learning vital to the success of companies. Organizational learning should include not only the training of employees but the transformation of the capabilities of the company and making learning an integral part of the strategic agenda.

### 16.5.2  Individual differences in learning

Not all people have the same facility to learn. Ironically, many times the best professionals have a tough time learning because they have not had the opportunity to gain experience from failures. People should learn from their mistakes and apply remedies, but they should also reflect on the validity of their prejudices and beliefs and be critical of their own behavior, modifying it if necessary.

### 16.5.3  Knowledge management

Learning organizations must develop specific skills and processes to improve and increase the level of knowledge of their employees and efficiently use that potential in the achievement of the organization's objectives (knowledge management). Knowledge management is the set of processes that facilitate access and timely use of knowledge that resides in people and / or in the informational structure of organizations to generate value, through problem solving, productivity increases, quality improvements, innovations in products, services, or factors of production. The activities normally contained in a knowledge management process are the following:

- Capture, create, encode, and organize knowledge, both tacit and explicit, in its different forms, so that users can easily access it.
- Transfer, apply and improve knowledge, through multiple channels, depending on the type of knowledge involved, so that it translates into the materialization of value propositions and continuous improvement.
- Preserve, protect, measure, and evaluate the impact and efficiency of knowledge management in value addition.

Although knowledge management is not just an information technology project, it is necessary to recognize that there are a lot of technological tools to support knowledge management. Among them we can distinguish three broad categories:

- Information repositories (digital libraries, online information services, document management systems).

- Resource directories (expert databases, integrated knowledge maps).
- Collaborative tools (email, virtual discussion forums).

Communities of practice are social tools for sharing knowledge in organizations; however, knowledge management thrives in a chaotic environment, trying to control it would be too rigid and truncate its growth.

## 16.6 RECOMMENDED READING

- Argyris, C. (1991) Teaching smart people how to learn. Harvard Business Review, HBR Special Issue, Winter 2019, pp. 60-71.
- Dodgson, M. & Gann, D. (2010). Innovation: A very short introduction. Oxford University Press.
- Gray, P., Cross, R. & Arena, M. (2022). Use networks to drive culture change. Sloan Management Review, Winter 2022.
- Kotter, J. (2007). Leading change: Why transformation efforts fail. Harvard Business Review, January 2007, pp. 96-103.
- Lundberg, A. and Westerman, G. (2020). The transformer CLO. Harvard Business Review, January- February 2020, pp. 84-93.

- Michels, D. & Murphy, K. (2021). How good is your company at change? Harvard Business Review, July- August 2021, pp. 62-71.
- Perry-Smith, J E. (2022). How collaboration needs change from mind to marketplace. Sloan Management Review, Winter 2022.
- Podolny, J. and Hansen, M.T. (2020). How Apple is organized for innovation. Harvard Business Review, November- December 2020, pp. 87-95.
- Silva, A. (2014). How to become an innovative company: A case study. International Journal of Innovation Science, Volume 6, Number 3, 2014, pp. 177-181.
- Siren, P.M. A., Anthony, S. D. & Bhatt, U. (2022). Persuade your company to change before it is too late. Harvard Business Review, January- February 2022, pp. 49-53.
- Thomke, S. (2020). Building a culture of experimentation. Harvard Business Review, March- April 2020, pp. 40-48.

# 17 ORGANIZATIONAL DESIGN

## 17.1 ORGANIZATIONAL DESIGN

An organization is a group of people and means ordered to a certain end. Organizational design is the project or configuration of all the elements or components of an organization. There is no single or better way to design a company. The design must be appropriate to the company in question.

Strategy precedes design and it is design that must align with strategy. Once the company defines what it wants and how it intends to achieve it, it can design or redesign the organization so that it responds to the strategy and allows the strategy's effective implementation.

Richard Daft, a professor of management at Vanderbilt University, argued that organizational design has two types of dimensions or components:

**Structural dimensions**: manuals or formal documents, specialization, or subdivision of tasks, who reports to whom, decision-making authority at each hierarchical level, level of formal education and training of employees, number of employees in each function or department.

**Contextual dimensions**: size of the organization, organizational technology, environment, goals and strategies of the organization, organizational culture.

When designing the organization, managers should answer questions like these:

- What are the company's goals and what are the strategies we need to implement to achieve those goals?
- What are the organizational activities that contribute most to the company's strategy and constitute sources of competitive advantage?
- Which organizational structure should we choose and how can we compensate for its disadvantages?
- What kind of leadership and culture we need to achieve the company's goals?

## 17.2 THE ORGANIZATIONAL STRUCTURE

Organizational structuring is the process to divide, organize, and coordinate the activities of an organization. According to Daft, there are three key components to defining organizational structure:

- Formal command relations, number of hierarchical levels, and control scope (number of report workers) of managers and supervisors.

- Grouping of individuals into departments and of these in the total organization.
- Design of systems to ensure communication, coordination, and effective integration of efforts in all departments.

The definition of organizational structure is not the only activity of organizational design, but it is often confused with it. In any case, the organizational structure is the framework that supports the company.

### 17.2.1 The best organizational structure

The best organizational structure for a company is the one that best suits its own characteristics.

### 17.2.2 The requirements of the organizational structure

- The structure must harmonize with the other elements or components of the company (strategy, technology, systems, people, management, culture).
- The structure must be appropriate to the size of the company.

- The structure must consider the type of company, the different businesses in which it may be involved, its products and services, and the geographical areas in which it operates.
- Structure is important, but it is not the determining factor of the success or failure of the company.

## 17.2.3 Types of organizational structures

The most common types of organizational structures are as follows:

- **Simple structure.** This structure has only one manager and a core of workers that he personally directs. It is the typical structure of any small business run by its sole owner.
- **Bureaucratic structure.** This structure establishes a clear hierarchy, a division of labor, and a set of formal rules and specialization.
- **Functional structure.** In a functional structure, the company is organized by functions. The typical functions are marketing, finance and operations or production, also distinguishing support functions such as planning and administration of human resources.

- **Divisional or multi divisional structure.** In this structure, the organization – called a corporation – establishes different divisions that are responsible for certain products, services, customer groups or geographical areas.
- **Matrix structure.** Type of organization by groups or work teams, in which employees can report to two or more bosses.
- **Virtual structure.** It is based on multiple network links between employees and teams, using communications technology.

### 17.2.4 The choice of type of structure

- If a company is small or medium-sized, a functional structure (marketing and sales departments, operations, finance, and human resources) suits it better. Only large companies need a more complicated organization.
- If a company has many products or services, it may be convenient to group them by categories and create operations departments for each of them and eventually business units or different companies to manage each of the company's businesses.

- Depending on the sector or industry in which it operates, a company may be able to adopt a structure similar to that of other companies in the same sector or industry. For example, banks, oil companies, and power companies usually have similar structures to those of other companies in the respective sector or industry.
- If a company has an internationalization strategy, it can start by creating a department to manage its international business and eventually create affiliates or subsidiaries to manage the business in each country or region in which it operates.
- If the company's strategy is to have a better relationship with its customers, then it must design its structure so that there are units or departments responsible for each group of customers and must adopt technologies that allow it to improve its relationships with customers or consumers.
- If the company's strategy is innovation, then it must ensure that its structure, rules, and procedures favor the free exchange of ideas and initiatives, its managers promote discussion and experimentation, its employees participate and

adapt easily to changes and there are units or groups dedicated to research and development.
- If a company is a consultant (engineering, management, or technology), it suits a matrix structure, assigning people to one or more projects while maintaining their relationship with the department or unit to which they belong.

### 17.2.5 Process-based design

The definition of the organizational structure should include the analysis of the work processes, to guarantee the proper coordination and integration of the activities of the different units of the company.

### 17.2.6 The change of structure is not the solution to all the problems of the company

Often, companies believe that the solution to their problems lies in a change of structure, but usually the fault lies elsewhere (strategy, management, people, processes, and systems). That is, the structure is important and must be appropriate to the characteristics of the company, but it is not convenient to change it continuously assuming that with that the company will work better.

## 17.3 THE SIZE OF THE ORGANIZATION AND THE LIFE CYCLE

Virtually all companies are born small. Some disappear, remain small or grow little, but others grow a lot. In the United States, a small company has fewer than five hundred workers and a large company has more than that number. Large corporations can have hundreds of thousands of workers and even millions, such as Walmart and the China National Petroleum Corporation.

Companies can grow for many reasons: to better serve their clientele, if it grows or even becomes global; acquire the number of resources needed to compete on a global scale; remain economically healthy; or deal with major projects. Other companies prefer to remain small to maintain greater responsiveness, greater flexibility in rapidly changing markets, have better control of the company, and provide a more humane work environment. Some try to be big but at the same time operate as if they were small, dividing the company into separate businesses.

In any case, companies usually have a life cycle initiated by a period in which they usually grow to the desired size and, in parallel, they go from an informal, non-bureaucratic environment, to a more bureaucratic and finally very bureaucratic one, although some try to make efforts to reduce bureaucracy. Then there is usually a period of decline, reducing the size of the company until it ends with its dissolution, unless efforts to maintain successful organizational performance are effective.

In general, about half of companies fail to survive after the first five years, but if they they manage to do so they usually last ten years or more. Very few companies manage to operate for more than one hundred years; apart from some very long-standing Japanese and European companies, General Electric, Coca Cola, Target, JCPenney, UPS, Neiman Marcus, and Boeing, among others, have remained active for more than one hundred years.

## 17.4 RECOMMENDED READING

- Anand, N., and Daft, R. L. (2007). What is the right organizational design? Organizational Dynamics, Vol. 36, No. 4, pp. 329–344.
- Daft, R.L. (2020). Organization theory and design. Cengage Learning, 13th Edition.

# 18 PROJECT MANAGEMENT

## 18.1 THE NOTION OF PROJECT

A project is a set of interrelated activities, performed in a set time, with the purpose of achieving a certain product or objective. Unlike a process, which is usually a continuous and repetitive activity, a project is a unique activity and has a beginning and an end.

Developing a new product is a project. But these are also projects: the development of an innovative marketing campaign; the adoption of an added information system; the construction of a building or a new plant; the execution of an important process of organizational change; the start of operations in another country; or the creation of a new business.

Some companies only do projects, usually for other companies or clients, for example, engineering and construction companies, advertising agencies, and consulting firms. However, most companies rely on processes for their day-to-day operations and undertake a project only when they want to make a change or create something new.

## 18.2 THE SELECTION OF PROJECTS

The projects demand a lot of attention, support, and

resources from the company, so it must carefully select the projects it undertakes. Evaluation of projects allow to determine their feasibility, alignment with strategy and contribution to the company's results. Companies should avoid too many projects running simultaneously, so it is necessary to prioritize them and discard or postpone those that are less profitable, necessary, or urgent.

## 18.3 PROJECT MANAGEMENT

Projects have displaced processes as the economic engine of our times. However, many companies still underestimate projects and project management, so only 35% of the projects conducted in the world are successful, representing a huge waste of time, money, and opportunities. Therefore, companies need to reinvent their project management approaches, adopting an organizational structure to drive projects, ensuring that their executives can sponsor projects, and training their managers in modern project management.

Project management is the function of planning, organizing, and executing a project. In some cases, the existing departments of the company can conduct the projects, but many times, especially if they are major or complex projects, it is necessary to establish temporary organizations to carry them out or hire a company to take care of the project. However, whether internal or external to the executing organization, there should be a project manager or leader and project team members.

The fundamental responsibility of the project manager is to conduct the project within the demands of time, cost, and quality. The proper selection of the project manager is the most crucial decision a company must make to ensure the desired results in a project. In general, the project manager must be a professional with experience in the exercise of this function, according to the size and complexity of the project, and must receive all the necessary authority to direct it. In large projects there could be a team leader, who is directly accountable to the project manager. In small projects, the project manager plays both roles.

## 18.4 THE PROCESS OF EXECUTING A PROJECT

The life cycle of a project is the sequence of phases of the development or execution of a project from its inception to its closure. In general, the process of executing a project follows the following phases:

- **Planning**. In this phase, project planners define the problem to be solved, identify the stakeholders, establish the objectives of the project, and determine the scope, resources, and main tasks.

To describe the scope and the main tasks of the project, it is convenient to define the work breakdown structure (WBS), which consists of the identification of the main parts or components that constitute the final product or products of the project. Additionally, at the beginning of the project, those responsible of the project must identify the risks that may cause the project to fail, determining the measures to avoid those risks or minimize their impact.

- **Development**. In this phase, the project began by creating the team, assigning tasks to each group or team member, creating the project schedule or calendar, preparing the budget, and starting the project.
- **Execution**. In this phase, the project manager leads the implementation of the project plan and control its execution, taking the necessary decisions to correct deviations, solve problems, and ensure that the project meets its objectives in time and with the established Budget.
- **Termination or closure**. This phase includes the completion of the project, the evaluation of its results, the administrative closure of the project, and the compilation of the lessons learned.

In most projects the phases are in a sequential manner (in cascade), although in some projects some superimposing may happen to accelerate the execution (fast track). However, in software development projects it is usual to use the Agile methodology, which follows an iterative process instead of sequential; that is, repeating several times the process, and using the results of each iteration as a starting point for the next iteration.

## 18.5 THE DURATION, COST AND QUALITY OF THE PROJECT

Three elements that require particular attention in the planning, development and execution of a project are its duration, cost, and quality.

### 18.5.1 The duration of a project

To estimate the duration, the project scope is needed. The scope of the project includes the following elements: the problem the project must solve; the mission of the project; the objectives of the project; the products required; the specifications of the products; and the work breakdown structure (WBS).

The work breakdown structure allows the definition of the activities for obtaining each of the products of the project. Once the project planners define the activities, the dependencies between them must be determined, that is, specify which activities must precede others and which to execute concurrently. Then the planners will estimate the duration or time needed to perform each of them.

As the project planners subdivide it into phases and activities, some schedule tool could express the sequence, interrelation, and opportunity of execution of each of them, to measure their compliance and execute the necessary adjustments. The schedule is a diagram that shows the duration and location in time of the different activities necessary to execute the project. The schedule should indicate the milestones or checkpoints that will allow us to evaluate the progress of the project and verify compliance with the plan. This tool is usually a chart or graph, distinguishing between bar charts or Gantt charts and network charts or PERT charts. The bar chart is useful for showing stakeholders and end users how the project is progressing, while the network diagram or flowchart may be better at managing activities and communicating detailed information to supervisors and people who are doing the work. Most projects use software to make the network diagrams and then control the execution of the project.

## 18.5.2  The cost of the project

The resources required are the people, equipment, materials, and facilities necessary for the execution of the project. Once the necessary resources in the project are known, as well as their magnitude and distribution over time, in correspondence with the project schedule, it follows the estimation of costs corresponding to these resources. The project planners should review and adjust the cost estimate as the project develops. The margin of error in this estimate, of course, will decrease as the project progresses and more accurate information about the resources needed and their cost become available.

## 18.5.3  Quality in the project

Quality is to meet the requirements specified by the client and accepted by the executing organization of the project.

Quality planning includes the identification of quality standards applicable to the project, including the quality policies and procedures of the project executing organization, as well as the definition of procedures for quality control in the project and the prevention of errors in the project products.

The products of the project must not have any defects; that is, no imperfection or lack of any of the qualities of the product. Prevention is about ensuring that defects do not occur. For effective prevention, it is necessary to start by establishing clear requirements and defining proven work processes.

## 18.6 DIFFICULTIES IN PROJECT IMPLEMENTATION

Even if there is a good plan to conduct the project, implementing it always results in a series of difficulties that exceed the forecasts at the planning stage. These difficulties can cover all the distinct aspects of the project. Among the difficulties that often arise when trying to implement a project are the following:

- Unforeseen events or pressures to include activities and products not contemplated in the initial scope.
- Project takes longer than anticipated.
- Costs incurred exceed those foreseen in the budget.
- Problems arise within the work team.

## 18.7 PROJECT SUCCESS FACTORS

To prevent conflicts and ensure the success of the project, the following elements are necessary:

- A good definition and understanding of customer requirements.
- A fair contract that specifies very well the scope of the project and the mechanisms for resolving conflicts or disputes that may arise.
- The appointment of a good manager and project team.
- Clear agreement on project goals between team members and customer representatives.
- A plan that shows the sequence of activities, defines clear responsibilities, and allows to measure progress during project execution.
- A good analysis of the risks that may affect the results of the project, including the definition of measures to avoid them or minimize their impact
- Effective and constant communication between everyone who participates in the project
- Corporate management support.

## 18.8 RECOMMENDED READING

- Davis, A. (2017). Projects: A very short introduction. Oxford University Press.
- Harvard Business Review (2020). Agile. Insights you need from Harvard Business Review.

- Harvard Business Review Press (2014). Managing projects. 20 minute manager series, Harvard Business School Publishing Corporation.
- Kerzner, H. (2022). Project management. Wiley, 13th Edition.
- Nieto- Rodriguez, A. (2021). The project economy has arrived. Harvard Business Review, pp. 38-45.
- Nieto- Rodriguez, A. (2021). Project management handbook: How to launch, lead, and sponsor successful projects. Harvard Business Review Press.
- Project Management Institute (2021). A guide to the project management body of knowledge (PMBOK guide). PMI, 7th Edition.

# 19 STRATEGY

## 19.1 THE CONCEPT OF STRATEGY

Strategy is the set of actions to achieve a goal. This is a term of military origin, which for a long time referred to the actions necessary to win a war, but is applied in many other areas, especially in politics and business, and its use continues to imply the idea that there is a rival or competitor who does not want us to achieve our goal and, therefore, the strategy is to define how to overcome that adversary.

## 19.2 STRATEGIC THINKING AND MANAGEMENT

The beginnings of strategic thinking are in Sun Tzu's "The Art of War," written about 2,500 years ago. Although all businesses, since the earliest times, have had to develop strategies to achieve their goals, the concept evolved after World War II. In the 1960s we can locate the beginning of strategic management, that is, the process of formulating and implementing the strategy of a company so that it can achieve the desired objectives, and the theories to support and guide that process.

## 19.3 SCHOOLS OF STRATEGIC MANAGEMENT

In the study of strategic management, following the classification proposed by Professor Henry Mintzberg, of McGill University in Canada, various schools or currents of thought have appeared:

- **The cognitive school**, which assumes that strategy formulation is a cognitive process that takes place in the strategist's mind.
- **The school of design**, which considers the formulation of strategy as a design process based on the determination of opportunities and threats (external analysis) and strengths and weaknesses (internal analysis).
- **The school of planning**, which involves the formulation of strategy as a detailed formal planning process.
- **The school of informal strategy evolution**, in favor of informal strategy evolution within the organization, in opposition to or as a complement to a deliberate process of strategy formulation.
- **The school of positioning**, which highlights the importance of the strategic positioning of the company in certain contexts, developing a competitive advantage over its rivals.

- **The theory of resources and capabilities**, which states that the competitive advantage of a company depends on the availability of resources that are not available to its competitors

Although companies still use all the above approaches, most have lost their validity and today the school of positioning and the theory of resources and capabilities, related to the concept of competitive advantage, prevail. Michael Porter, a professor at Harvard University, and Jay Barney, a professor at the University of Utah, have been the main authors, respectively, in those two schools or theories.

## 19.4 STRATEGIC ANALYSIS

Not all approaches require it, but in general it is convenient to conduct a strategic analysis, to determine the current situation of the company, and use that analysis to formulate the strategy. Strategic analysis has two components: external analysis and internal analysis.

### 19.4.1 External analysis

External analysis is the consideration of the main forces of the environment that can influence the management of the company. As a result of the external analysis, opportunities, and threats of the environment for the company must be determined. Some external analysis techniques are as follows:

- Trend analysis.
- Simulation or analysis of scenarios.
- PESTEL analysis (analysis of political, economic, social, technological, environmental, and legal factors).
- Analysis of the seven factors (markets and consumers, competition, economy, government and regulation, social and demographic factors, technology, and factors of production).
- Analysis of industry or sector forces.

The analysis of the forces of the industry or sector, proposed by Michael Porter, involves the consideration of the following forces:

- Threats from new entrants.
- Threats of substitute products or services.
- Bargaining power of suppliers.
- Bargaining power of consumers or buyers.
- Intensity of rivalry between existing companies.

### 19.4.2 Internal analysis

Internal analysis is the evaluation of the internal situation of the company, in all its functional areas and in the relationships between these areas. It aims to determine the strengths and weaknesses of the company.

Some of the internal analysis techniques are as follows:

- Analysis of key business functions.
- Value chain model.
- Model of the 7s or Mc Kinsey model.
- Process improvement.
- Importance-performance matrix.
- Competitive positioning.
- Portfolio analysis.
- Assessment of core competencies.
- Diagnosis of the organization's capacity for change.

The value chain model, also proposed by Michael Porter, involves distinguishing between:

- Primary activities or internal activities that provide value to the customer (logistics, operations, marketing and sales, after-sales service).
- Secondary activities, which support primary activities (company infrastructure, human resource management, technological development, supply).

- The internal analysis, using this model, consists of evaluating each activity in relation to its function in the value chain.

## 19.5 STRATEGY OPTIONS

Companies have a wide variety of strategies, among which they must choose according to their situation (opportunities, threats, strengths, weaknesses):

- **Generic strategies.** They aim to gain a competitive advantage through cost leadership (low price), differentiation, or specialization.
- **Offensive strategies.** They eliminate or weaken competition. Examples: offering products with lower price or higher quality; aggressive penetration in underserved market segments; establishment of plants near markets; acquisition of control over raw materials or distribution channels necessary for competition.
- **Deterrence strategies.** They aim to establish barriers to entry for new competitors. Examples: remarkably high investments in advertising or in facilities and equipment; financial strengthening; development of innovative technologies.

- **Defensive strategies.** They respond to attacks from competitors. Examples: price reduction; investment in marketing and advertising; quality improvement; innovation; aggression against the opponent in another market; conducting preemptive strikes; changing market segment; cutting expenses; selling parts of the company; liquidation or exit from the market.
- **Cooperation strategies or alliances.** They aim to combine efforts with other companies to compete more effectively. Examples: license exchange; joint marketing agreements; manufacture of products for another company; long-term agreements for obtaining inputs; consortia; setting manufacturing standards; joint research agreements; franchises; joint ventures or joint ventures; mergers. Merger occurs when two companies decide to join forces to be one, and acquisition happens when one company buys another.
- **Integration strategies.** They aim to increase control over distributors, suppliers, and competition. Forward integration is control over distributors, backward integration is control over suppliers,

and horizontal integration is control over competition.
- **Diversification strategies.** They aim to add new products or services. In general, diversification is based on products or services of common characteristics, in which the company has a better strategic position, and the market is in a growth phase. Synergy is the benefit derived from combining two or more businesses or lines of products or services, so that the combined performance is greater than the sum of the performance of the individual businesses.
- **Internationalization strategies.** They aim to take advantage of business opportunities in other countries. They present opportunities for profit but also risks. The competitiveness of the company will determine its success in international markets.

It is not always easy to choose the most convenient strategy or strategies and it is likely that changes or adjustments happen on the fly. For the same reason, there is no single strategy that is always the best; however, in the business field usually the best strategy is differentiation, that is, doing something different from what competitors do so that consumers can prefer the product or service that one intends to sell them.

The main source of competitive advantage is a strategy that competitors cannot easily imitate. This makes innovation, which is the basis of differentiation, at the heart of modern business strategy. However, an innovation strategy or any other isolated strategy is usually not enough. A holistic strategic approach integrates carefully chosen options in relation to the business model, competitive position, implementation processes that continuously adapt to the changing environment, and the capabilities needed to win in the long term.

Companies that have multiple products may choose different strategies for them depending on, among other factors, the growth rate of the industry each product is in, and the market share of the product. In general, products that have a high market share but are in a low-growth market can generate profits that help drive market share of products that are in high-growth markets.

## 19.6 THE IMPLEMENTATION OF THE STRATEGY

In the beginnings of strategic management, in the first decades of the second half of the twentieth century, the emphasis was on the planning stage. Keeping with a little changing environment, companies thought that what was necessary was to elaborate a detailed long-term strategic plan, updated periodically, with precise implementation instructions to the different departments of the company.

Towards the end of that century, particularly in its last decade, the global environment became very dynamic, and changes of all kinds (political, economic, social, legal) became increasingly frequent and unpredictable, with the result that detailed long-term strategic plans became impractical and companies found it necessary to rely on general strategic guidelines, implemented through improvisation and adaptation to the new realities. That is, implementation became as or more important than strategic planning.

Implementing or executing strategy is a complex and arduous process, especially in large corporations even if strategies are correctly formulated.

The successful execution of the strategy depends on the effective direction of the process by the top leader of the company and the compatibility between the strategy and the other components of the company. When implementing the strategy, the company must ensure that it is compatible with the other components of the organization: structure; people; technology; essential skills; culture; and management style.

In addition to the effective direction of the process and the compatibility of the strategy with the other components of the company, the successful execution of the strategy depends on:

- Efficient allocation of resources.
- Establishing appropriate policies and procedures.
- Using management tools to control the process.
- The establishment of a favorable organizational climate.
- The use of appropriate rewards and incentives.

## 19.7 MONITORING THE IMPLEMENTATION OF THE STRATEGY

When implementing the strategy, it is necessary to use some control system to check the progress and establish the necessary adjustments or corrections. One such system is the balanced scorecard.

The balanced scorecard uses performance indicators from four perspectives:

- Finance (shareholders).
- Clients.
- Internal processes.
- Learning and change.

The elaboration of the balanced scorecard involves

the construction of a strategic tree or cause-effect diagram, establishing the causal relationships between the strategies corresponding to the different perspectives, usually through the sequence:

Learning and change → Internal processes → Clients → Finance (shareholders).

## 19.8 RECOMMENDED READING

- Barney, J. (2001). Resource- based theories of competitive advantage: A ten-year retrospective of the resource-based view. Journal of Management, 27 (2001) 643-650.
- Collis, D.J. (2021). Why do so many strategies fail? Harvard Business Review, July- August 2021, pp. 82-93.
- Daub, C. (2020). Business strategy: Essentials you always wanted to know. Vibrant Publishers.
- Ghiglione, F. A. (2021). The balanced scorecard as a tool for efficiency in business management. Administrative Sciences, Digital Journal FCE- UNLP, Year 9, No. 18, July- December 2021, pp. 87- 93
- Mintzberg, H. & Lampel, J. (1999). Reflecting on the strategy process. Sloan Management Review, Spring 1999, pp. 21-30.

- Porter, M. (1996). What is strategy? Harvard Business Review, November-December 1996, pp. 61-78.
- Sun Tzu (fifth century BC/2021). The art of war. Independently published, Amazon.

# 20 TECHNOLOGY

## 20.1 TECHNOLOGY MANAGEMENT

Technology management is the function of developing and updating the systems that allow us to effectively manage the information in the company and efficiently conduct the production and marketing processes.

## 20.2 THE IMPORTANCE OF TECHNOLOGY IN BUSINESS

Technology in business is a growing need. As time goes on, the business world is becoming more technological. Innovation nurtures business, and as technology creates the appropriate path for the development of innovation, we can say that businesses need technology to sustain themselves.

Technology has a significant impact on business operations. No matter the size of the company, technology can bring many benefits that will help you earn higher revenue. The key role of technology in business is to drive growth and improve operations. Without technology, companies will certainly fail to stay afloat in today's competitive and globalized market.

The degree to which a company invests in technology correlates directly and significantly with its high productivity and competitiveness by reducing its operating costs, improving the quality of its products, and even improving the working conditions of employees and workers. Technological innovation is a key factor in industrial evolution, economic development, and international competitiveness.

## 20.3 TYPES OF BUSINESS TECHNOLOGY

The technologies companies use encompass a wide variety of equipment and systems ranging from phones, cars, trucks, computers, and networks to robots and process control systems. However, there are three types of systems of significant importance for the productivity of companies:

- Information systems.
- Communication systems.
- Production support systems.

### 20.3.1 Information systems

Companies can have several information systems, like the following:

- **Transaction processing systems**. Transactions encompass all purchases and sales of products and services, along with any daily business transactions or activity required to operate a business. The amounts and types of transactions may vary, depending on the industry and the size/scope of the company. Examples of typical transactions are customer billing, bank deposits, new hire data, or a data record of customer relationships. A transaction processing system ensures the storage of all contractual, transactional and customer relationship data in a secure location, accessible to all who need it. It also assists in the processing of sales order entries, payroll, shipping, sales management, or other routine transactions necessary to maintain operations.

- **Office automation systems.** An office automation system is a network of various tools, technologies, and people needed to conduct administrative and management tasks. Typical examples of functions performed by these systems include printing documents, mailing documents, maintaining a company calendar, and producing reports. An office automation system helps to improve communication between different departments so that everyone can collaborate to complete a task.

- **Knowledge management systems**. A knowledge management system stores and extracts information to help users improve their knowledge and optimize collaborative efforts to complete tasks. Some examples of documents found in a knowledge management system include employee training materials, company policies and procedures, or answers to customer questions.
- **Management information systems**. A management information system uses various transaction data to help middle managers optimize planning and decision-making. Retrieves information from transaction processing systems, aggregates it, and generates reports to help those at the management level know key details of a situation. Summaries and comparisons allow senior managers to optimize the decision-making process to achieve better results. Most report formats encompass summaries of annual sales data, performance data, or historical records. This provides a secure and systematized way for managers to meet their goals and oversee business units.
- **Decision support systems**. A decision support system (DSS) processes data to aid in management

decision making. It stores and collects the information necessary for management to take the right action at the right time. For example, a bank manager may use such a system to assess changing lending trends and determine which annual lending goals to meet. Decision support systems allow you to analyze and summarize substantial amounts of information and put it into a visual element that makes it understandable. Because these systems are interactive, management can easily add or remove data and ask important questions. This provides the evidence necessary for middle management to make the right decisions that will ensure the company meets its objectives.

- **Executive support systems.** Executive support systems are like a decision support system but used by executive leaders and owners to optimize decision-making. An expert system helps business leaders find answers to non-routine questions so they can make decisions that improve the company's prospects and performance. Unlike a decision support system, an executive support system supplies better telecommunications functionality and greater computing functionality.

Graphics software within such a system display data on tax regulations, competitive startups, internal compliance issues, and other relevant executive information. This allows leaders to track internal performance, monitor competition, and identify growth opportunities.

- **Integrated systems**. Companies use commercial information systems that they can acquire and install in isolation, to perform or support specific processes, or they can take advantage of the technological resources available through integrated information systems or enterprise resource planning (ERP) systems. These systems are a set of computer program modules that allow the automation and linking of organizational functions such as accounting, finance, purchasing, human resources, production, and distribution, among others.
- **Management systems for relations with consumers**. A consumer relationship management (CRM) system is a process in which a company manages its interactions with consumers or customers, typically using data analytics to study substantial amounts of information. Such a system uses information from transaction processing systems

integrated into an enterprise resource planning (ERP) system.

### 20.3.2 Communication systems

Companies can make use of many types of systems to facilitate communication between their employees, suppliers, distributors, and customers, including websites, email systems, social networks, and systems for supporting meetings and teamwork.

### 20.3.3 Production support systems

As part of the growing use of technology for business management, industrial technology is evolving towards the complete digitalization of production operations and the integration of all systems. In addition to CAD/CAM systems (computer support for design and manufacturing) and automation and process control systems, many companies use innovative technologies such as robotics, analytics, artificial intelligence, cognitive technologies, nanotechnology, and the Internet of Things, among others.

## 20.4 NEW TECHNOLOGIES

Innovative technologies, particularly artificial

intelligence, will redefine management. All companies, traditional and modern, need to understand the revolutionary impact of artificial intelligence on their operations, strategy, and competitiveness. Managers who want to be effective in the future will have to rely on artificial intelligence in all their activities, including strategy formulation, monitoring, coordination, control, and decision-making. They must ensure that artificial intelligence is the main source of value creation and delivery. They will also need to strengthen their social and relationship skills, for which artificial intelligence will be less supportive.

## 20.5 THE CHALLENGES OF TECHNOLOGY

Despite the extraordinary advantages of having modern information technologies, the necessary investment in computer equipment and systems is high, as well as the cost of software licenses and the cost of training employees to effectively use innovative technologies, posing a significant challenge to managers' ability to efficiently take advantage of these resources. Innovative technologies are not necessarily a good thing unless used effectively.

Additionally, managers face significant issues related to threats to the security of systems and the protection of company data and customer data. Security and privacy have complicated the management of information systems.

## 20.6 RECOMMENDED READING

- Amabile, T. (2020). Creativity, artificial intelligence, and a world of surprises. Academy of Management Discoveries, Vol. 6, No. 3, pp. 351–354.
- Boden, M. A. (2018). Artificial intelligence: A very short introduction. Oxford University Press.
- Davenport, T. H. (2019). The AI advantage: How to put the artificial intelligence revolution to work. The MIT Press.
- Editor's comments (2020). Special issue editorial: Artificial intelligence in organizations: Current estate and future opportunities. MIS Quarterly Executive, December 2020, 19:4, pp. ix- xxi.
- Iansiti, M., and Lakhani, K. R. (2020). Competing in the age of AI. Harvard Business Review, January- February 2020, pp. 61- 67.
- Kolbjørnsrud, V., Amico, R. & Thomas, R. J. (2016). How artificial intelligence will redefine management. Harvard Business Review, November 2, 2016.

www.ingramcontent.com/pod-product-compliance
Lightning Source LLC
Chambersburg PA
CBHW020637220526
45464CB00001B/191